Getting Uncle Sam to Enforce Your Civil Rights

United States Commission on Civil Rights
Clearinghouse Publication 59
Revised December 2007

U.S. Commission on Civil Rights

The U.S. Commission on Civil Rights is an independent, bipartisan agency established by Congress in 1957. It is directed to:

- Investigate complaints alleging that citizens are being deprived of their right to vote by reason of their race, color, religion, sex, age, disability, or national origin, or by reason of fraudulent practices.
- Study and collect information relating to discrimination or a denial of equal protection of the laws under the Constitution because of race, color, religion, sex, age, disability, or national origin, or in the administration of justice.
- Appraise federal laws and policies with respect to discrimination or denial of equal protection of the laws because of race, color, religion, sex, age, disability, or national origin, or in the administration of justice.
- Serve as a national clearinghouse for information in respect to discrimination or denial of equal protection of the laws because of race, color, religion, sex, age, disability, or national origin.
- Submit reports, findings, and recommendations to the President and Congress.
- Issue public service announcements to discourage discrimination or denial of equal protection of the laws.

Members of the Commission

Gerald A. Reynolds, *Chairperson*
Abigail Thernstrom, *Vice Chairperson*
Jennifer C. Braceras
Gail Heriot
Peter N. Kirsanow
Arlan Melendez
Ashley L. Taylor, Jr.
Michael Yaki
Kenneth L. Marcus, *Staff Director*

U.S. Commission on Civil Rights
624 Ninth Street, NW
Washington, DC 20425
(202) 376-8128 voice
(800) 877-8339 TTY
www.usccr.gov

Getting Uncle Sam to Enforce Your Civil Rights

Letter from the Staff Director

Dear Reader,

Getting Uncle Sam to Enforce Your Civil Rights is a comprehensive resource for the American public that explains where and how an aggrieved individual can file a discrimination claim. The U.S. Commission on Civil Rights publishes this guide to aid the public in accessing entities responsible for civil rights enforcement. The Commission lacks enforcement powers to apply remedies in individual cases; however, it refers many of the complaints it receives to the appropriate federal, state, or local government agencies, or private organizations that are authorized to help.

This publication is one of many that the Commission issues as part of its duty to serve as a national clearinghouse for information about discrimination or denial of equal protection of the laws because of race, color, religion, sex, age, disability, or national origin. The Commission and its State Advisory Committees have produced and disseminated hundreds of reports, studies, and public service announcements on national, regional, and local civil rights matters. These include the Commission's *Civil Rights Journal*, published periodically, which contains articles on topical civil rights issues.

Copies of Commission publications, as well as a "Catalog of Publications," are available free to the public, by request to the Publications Office, U.S. Commission on Civil Rights, 624 Ninth Street, NW, Room 600, Washington, DC 20425. This is also the location of the Commission's Robert S. Rankin Civil Rights Memorial Library, which is open to the public during business hours on weekdays. In addition, many of the Commission's more recent publications, including this one, can be accessed on its Web site at www.usccr.gov. The Commission periodically updates the online version of this publication.

The Commission's reports and studies result from the agency's mandate to appraise federal civil rights laws and policies, investigate complaints of voting rights violations, and study and collect information relating to discrimination or a denial of equal protection of the laws. Fact-finding for carrying out these functions includes the holding of hearings, briefings, presentations, and forums in Washington and other locations around the country, to gather evidence and information for findings and reports. These Commission activities examine important civil rights issues of both national and local impact and are open to the public.

To obtain a referral, individuals may call the Commission's toll-free complaint line, or any of the Commission's six regional offices in Washington, DC; Atlanta; Chicago; Kansas City; Denver; and Los Angeles (see pages 3 and 101 of this publication). The Commission's regional offices coordinate local operations and assist the Commission's 51 State Advisory Committees (one for each state and the District of Columbia) in their activities. Advisory Committees are composed of volunteer citizens familiar with local and state civil rights issues who assist the Commission with fact-finding, investigation, and information dissemination.

The Commission is proud to issue this publication as a public service, and hopes that in so doing, all Americans will find it a useful and convenient resource for protecting and securing their civil rights.

Sincerely,

KENNETH L. MARCUS
Staff Director

Acknowledgments

This publication was produced by the Office of Civil Rights Evaluation, Robert Lerner, PhD, director. Principal research and editing were performed by Latrice D. Foshee.

vi

Contents

1. Introduction

There are many federal laws against discrimination. They were passed to protect people who, because of their race, color, religion, sex, national origin, age, or disability, are denied their rights.

Discrimination might occur when an individual attempts to vote; rent or buy a home; use a public facility; obtain a job, an education, or a bank loan; or do many other things.

Discrimination is illegal when an individual is denied an opportunity or a service based on:

- race, which is generally understood to be membership in a racial group. Depending on which law is involved, membership in an ethnic group can also constitute race;

- color, which refers to a person's actual skin shade, and may constitute a separate discrimination factor regardless of the person's race;

- sex, which refers to gender;

- religion, which refers to a person's religious beliefs and practices, or lack thereof, or a person's membership in a religious group;

- national origin, which refers to an individual's country of origin, the origin of an individual's ancestors, or the physical, cultural, or linguistic characteristics of a particular nationality. This includes characteristics such as last name, accent, and cultural heritage;

- age, which refers to persons aged 40 or over; or

- disability, which refers to physical or mental impairments that substantially limit one or more major life activities of an individual.

If you believe that you have been discriminated against and want to file a complaint with the federal government, this publication is intended to help you.

This publication will help you review your rights and guide you through the initial steps of filing a discrimination complaint; it will not inform you of all the steps involved in successfully pursuing the complaint after you have filed it. If you desire a detailed description of the overall process beyond the initial steps, further information can be obtained by contacting the federal, state, and local officials or one or more of the organizations listed in this publication.

How do you prepare a complaint? Where do you send it?

Before you file a discrimination complaint, you should seek more information from:

- trained legal counsel;

- federal, state, and local officials; and/or

- public service organizations referenced in this publication.

States, counties, and municipalities also have laws against discrimination, which sometimes provide different protection or relief. If they have laws that apply to your complaint, you may file with them instead of, or in addition to, filing with the federal government. The federal government has arrangements with some state and local governments to refer certain kinds of complaints to these localities for processing.

Among the federal laws that require people to be treated equally are the Equal Pay Act of 1963, the Civil Rights Acts of 1964 and 1991, the Voting Rights Act of 1965, Executive Order 11,246 (1965), as amended by Executive Order 11,375 (1967), the Age Discrimination in Employment Act of 1967, the Fair Housing Act of 1968, Title IX of the Education Amendments of 1972, the Rehabilitation Act of 1973, the Equal Credit Opportunity Act of 1974, the Equal Educational Opportunity Act of 1974, the Age Discrimination Act of 1975, the Individuals with Disabilities Education Act of 1975, the Community Reinvestment Act of 1977, the Immigration Reform and Control Act of 1986, the Civil Rights Restoration Act of 1987, Fair Housing Amendments Act of 1988, the Americans with Disabilities Act of 1990, Voting Rights Language Assistance Act of 1992, and the Family and Medical Leave Act of 1993.

Many federal agencies are responsible for enforcing these laws and the regulations to implement them. Some agencies require individuals to complete a complaint form before they act against an individual or organization that violates people's rights. Because laws and regulations frequently require that complaints be filed within certain time limits, **it is important to file immediately after the discriminatory act occurs**. While this publication provides telephone numbers, complainants are strongly encouraged to submit a written complaint, attaching copies of all pertinent information. At some point in the process, the agency most probably will require written documentation.

The U.S. Commission on Civil Rights (USCCR) has no power to enforce laws and, hence, cannot resolve individual complaints of discrimination. However, after reading this publication, if you are still uncertain what agency you should contact to file a complaint of discrimination, you may contact the Commission at the following address and we can assist you by referring your matter to the appropriate civil rights enforcement agency:

U.S. Commission on Civil Rights
Office of Civil Rights Evaluation
COMPLAINTS REFERRAL
624 Ninth Street, NW
Washington, DC 20425
(202) 376-8513
(800) 552-6843
TTY: (202) 376-8116
Fax: (202) 376-7754
www.referrals@usccr.gov

You may also contact the appropriate **USCCR** regional office. See page 94.

2. How to File a Complaint

Your complaint should be in writing, preferably typed or printed neatly, dated, signed, and should include the following information:

- your name;

- your address, and your home and work telephone numbers;

- the name(s) and address(es) of the person(s) and/or establishment you believe to have discriminated against you;

- a description of the act(s) of discrimination. This should include the date and place of the action(s), and what you believe to be the basis for discrimination (race, sex, etc.); and

- the name(s), address(es), and telephone number(s) of any person(s) with information concerning your complaint.

When your complaint is investigated, you may be asked to provide **copies** of receipts, contracts, or other records supporting your claim of discrimination. Any materials that you would want returned should not be sent with your initial complaint.

Generally, most government agencies require that complaints be postmarked within **180 days** of the discriminatory action. You should, however, inquire about specific deadlines that may apply to your case. Depending on your type of case or your status, you may be required to file your complaint earlier.

3. When and Where to File a Complaint

Some agencies handle complaints only at their Washington, DC, head-quarters; others process them through regional or local offices. Some handle them at both places. For more details, take note of any special instructions regarding the filing of complaints at the specific agencies listed throughout this publication.

Credit

Federal laws such as the Equal Credit Opportunity Act of 1974 and the Fair Housing Act of 1968, as amended, prohibit discrimination in providing credit or credit-related services. Both laws prohibit discrimination in residential real estate transactions, and the Equal Credit Opportunity Act also prohibits discrimination in consumer and business or commercial loans. In all credit transactions you are protected from discrimination that occurs on the basis of your race, color, religion, sex, marital status, age (provided the applicant has the capacity to contract), national origin, or receipt of public assistance, or because you have exercised a right under the Consumer Credit Protection Act. In credit transactions related to housing, you are also protected from discrimination because of family status or disability. According to these laws, when you apply for credit a creditor may not:

- discourage you from applying;

- ask you to reveal your gender, race, national origin, or religion. A creditor may ask you to voluntarily disclose this information if you are applying for a home loan. A creditor may also ask about your residence or immigration status;

- ask whether you are divorced or widowed;

- ask what is your marital status if you are applying for individual, unsecured credit, unless you live in a community property state;

- ask you for information about your husband or wife. A creditor may ask about your spouse, or former spouse, if: your spouse is applying with you; your spouse will be allowed to use the account; you are relying on your spouse's income or on alimony or child support income from a former spouse; or if you reside in a community property state;

- ask about your plans for having or rearing children; or

- ask if you receive alimony, child support, or separate maintenance payments.

When deciding whether to give you, credit a creditor may not:

- consider your gender, marital status, race, color, national origin, or religion;

- consider the race of the people who live in the neighborhood where you want to buy, or improve, a house with borrowed money; or

- consider your age, unless you are too young to sign a binding contract, generally under 18 years of age, or if the information is to be used to see whether your income will be reduced with retirement.

When evaluating your income, a creditor may not:

- refuse to consider public assistance income, alimony, child support, or separate maintenance payments if that income is received consistently;

- discount income because of your gender or marital status or on any basis for which discrimination is prohibited;

- discount or refuse to consider income derived from pension, annuity, or retirement benefits programs; or

- discount or refuse to consider income derived from part-time employment, but you may have to show that this income can be expected to continue.

You also have the right to:

- have the credit in your birth name, your first name, and your spouse's last name, or your first name and combined last names;

- obtain credit without a cosigner, if you meet the creditor's standards;

- have a cosigner other than your husband or wife, if one is necessary;

- keep your own account after you change your name, marital status, reach a certain age, or retire, unless the creditor has evidence that you are unable or unwilling to pay;

- know within 30 days of filing your application whether it has been accepted or rejected;

- know specifically why an application was rejected, since indefinite and vague reasons are illegal;

- learn the specific reasons why you were offered less favorable terms than those for which you applied; and

- receive copies of appraisal reports for credit that is to be secured by a dwelling.

If you think you have been discriminated against by a creditor:

- in being discouraged from applying for credit or a loan;

- in being given unfair terms for credit or a loan; or

- in being denied credit or a loan;

write to the agency in charge of enforcing the equal credit practices of that lender.

A creditor must give you the name and address of the appropriate enforcement agency when it turns down the terms you request or denies you credit. If a lender does not offer you this information or refuses to give it to you, write to the appropriate agency in the list that follows. These agencies may not resolve individual complaints, but they will use consumer comments to decide which companies to investigate.

You should also complain if you think a lender is "redlining"—refusing to make loans, or setting different conditions for loans, on property in a community because of the area's racial, religious, or ethnic population. When certain financial institutions try to get approval from their regulatory agency to:

- obtain federal deposit insurance;

- establish a facility authorized to receive deposits, or relocate an existing office;

- merge or consolidate with, or acquire another institution;

- acquire deposits from another institution; or

- form a bank or savings association holding company;

individuals and community groups have an opportunity to comment on whether the institution is redlining as an objection to its approval for the proposed transaction. You can request the regulatory agency to place you on its mailing list so you are aware of the comment period for:

- a nationally chartered bank (National or N.A. will be part of the name). Write to one of the district offices of the **Comptroller of the Currency** listed on page 52. For publications or additional information contact:

Comptroller of the Currency
Compliance Management
Independence Square
250 E Street, SW
Washington, DC 20219
(202) 874-5216
TTY: (202) 922-3275
www.occ.treas.gov

- a bank holding company or state-chartered bank that is a member of the **Federal Reserve System**. Write to one of the Federal Reserve Banks listed on page 73 or contact:

Board of Governors of the Federal Reserve System
Division of Consumer and Community Affairs
20th and C Streets, NW
Mail Stop 801
Washington, DC 20551-0001
(202) 452-3693
Fax: (202) 728-5850
www.federalreserve.gov

or

Board of Governors of the Federal Reserve System
Publications Services
20th and C Streets, NW
Mail Stop 127
Washington, DC 20551-0001
(202) 452-3245

- a state-chartered bank insured by the **Federal Deposit Insurance Corporation** (it will display the FDIC symbol) and not a member of the Federal Reserve System. Write to one of the regional offices on page 71 or to:

8

Federal Deposit Insurance Corporation
Consumer Affairs
550 17th Street, NW, Suite 5112
Washington, DC 20429
(202) 898-6601
(877) 275-3342
TDD: (800) 925-4618
www.fdic.gov

- a federally insured savings association or federally chartered savings bank. Write to one of the regional offices of the **Office of Thrift Supervision** on page 78 or to:

Office of Thrift Supervision
Consumer Programs
1700 G Street, NW
Washington, DC 20552
(202) 906-6237
(800) 842-6929
TTY: (800) 877-8339
Fax: (202) 906-6326
www.ots.treas.gov

Although federal credit unions are not subject to the Community Reinvestment Act, they must comply with fair lending laws and the nondiscrimination rules issued by their regulators. Forward any complaint to one of the regional offices of the **National Credit Union Administration** listed on page 77 or to:

National Credit Union Administration
1775 Duke Street, Suite 4206
Alexandria, VA 22314-3437
(703) 519-4600
TTY: (703) 518-6332
Fax: (703) 518-6429
www.ncua.gov

Complaints against a state-chartered credit union should be forwarded to the state office that oversees credit unions or to the **Federal Trade Commission** listed on page 11.

Complaints against an institution of the **U.S. Cooperative Farm Credit System**, such as farm credit banks, federal land bank associations, production credit associations, agricultural credit banks, federal land credit associations, and agricultural credit associations should be forwarded to:

Farm Credit Administration
Office of Congressional and Public Affairs
1501 Farm Credit Drive
McLean, VA 22102-5090
V/TTY: (703) 883-4056

Fax: (703) 790-3260
www.fca.gov

Complaints of discrimination in benefits or services provided by recipients of **Small Business Administration (SBA)** financial assistance or SBA program offices should be forwarded to:

U.S. Small Business Administration
Equal Employment Opportunity and Civil Rights Compliance
409 Third Street, SW, Suite 6400
Washington, DC 20416
(202) 205-6750
TTY: (202) 205-7150
Fax: (202) 205-7580
www.sba.gov

If you think you have been discriminated against in violation of the Fair Housing Act, contact one of the HUD enforcement centers listed on page 58 or:

U.S. Department of Housing and Urban Development
Fair Housing and Equal Opportunity
Office of Investigations
451 Seventh Street, SW, Room 5204
Washington, DC 20410-2000
(202) 619-8041
(202) 708-0836
Hot line: (800) 669-9777
TTY: (800) 927-9275
Fax: (202) 708-1425
www.hud.gov

Financial institutions have an obligation to meet the credit needs of your community, even though it may be characterized by low- or moderate-income residents. The Department of Justice handles discrimination complaints filed against all kinds of creditors. It may sue lenders who show a pattern or practice of equal credit opportunity violations, or file suit in cases referred to it by the agencies that initially investigate complaints. To contact the **Department of Justice**, call or write to:

U.S. Department of Justice
Civil Rights Division
Housing and Civil Enforcement Section
950 Pennsylvania Avenue, NW
Washington, DC 20530
(202) 514-4713
Fax: (202) 514-1116
www.usdoj.gov

For more information on discrimination in credit-lending and credit-related services, including information about bringing suit under the Equal Credit Opportunity Act, call the **Federal Trade Commission** or write to:

Federal Trade Commission
Consumer Response Center
Sixth Street and Pennsylvania Avenue, NW
Washington, DC 20580
(202) 326-3758
(202) 326-2222
Hot line: (877) 382-4357
TTY: (202) 326-2502
Fax: (202) 326-2050
www.ftc.gov

Education

According to federal laws that prohibit discrimination because of race, color, national origin, sex, age, or disability in programs that receive federal financial assistance, any program or activity that receives funds from the Department of Education must operate in a nondiscriminatory manner.

Any educational or other institution or facility that receives federal financial assistance may not discriminate on the basis of race, color, national origin, sex, disability, or age so as to:

- deny you or your child aid, a service, or a benefit afforded others;

- provide you or your child an inferior service;

- segregate you or your child on the basis of race, color, or national origin;

- segregate you or your child on the basis of sex, other than for contact sports or varsity athletic competition, or segregate you or your child on the basis of disability where such segregation is not educationally necessary;

- deny admission to schools or postsecondary institutions on the basis of race, color, national origin, or age, or generally, on the basis of sex except with regard to admission to religious undergraduate institutions;

- engage in conduct that has the effect of denying you or your child aid, a service, or a benefit, or otherwise discriminating against you or your child;

- deny or restrict you or your child's access to elementary, secondary, or vocational education because you are, or your child is, limited-English proficient;

- or otherwise treat you or your child adversely on the basis of race, color, national origin, gender, disability, or age.

Schools may not discriminate against students because of pregnancy, parenthood, or marital status. Such discrimination includes barring a student from classes or extracurricular activities or expulsion.

In sports, schools must provide equivalent treatment, services, and benefits to students of both sexes.

Civil rights laws protecting individuals from discrimination in programs (all activities of an institution) that receive federal funds extend to all state educational agencies, elementary and secondary school systems, colleges and universities, vocational schools, proprietary schools, state vocational rehabilitation agencies, libraries, and museums that receive federal financial assistance.

These programs may include, but are not limited to, admissions, recruitment, financial aid, academic programs, student treatment and services, counseling and guidance, discipline, classroom assignment, grading, vocational education, recreation, physical education, athletics, housing, and employment.

Federal antidiscrimination laws apply to the entire program even if the federal assistance affects only a small portion of the program.

In addition, Executive Order 13,160 prohibits discrimination based on race, sex, color, national origin, disability, religion, age, sexual orientation, and status as a parent in federally conducted education and training programs.

If you think you or your child has been discriminated against by a public school, college, or university, or a private school, college, or university that receives federal financial assistance, you may file a formal complaint against the institution receiving federal funds with the appropriate regional office of the **Office for Civil Rights (OCR) of the U.S. Department of Education** listed on page 53 or with:

U.S. Department of Education
Office for Civil Rights
330 C Street, SW, Suite 5000
Washington, DC 20202
(202) 205-5413
(800) 421-3481
(877) 521-2172
Fax: (202) 205-5381
www.ed.gov

The person or organization filing the complaint need not be a victim of the alleged discrimination, but may complain on behalf of another person or group.

The complaint must be filed within **180 calendar days** of the date of the alleged discrimination. However, if you already filed under the educational institution's grievance procedures, you will be allowed 60 days from the last act of the institution grievance process. Your formal complaint should include the information outlined in Chapter 2 and also state whether you think a whole group of students or teachers is being discriminated against.

Certain complaints should also be sent to the U.S. Attorney General, who may bring suit after receiving a written and signed complaint from:

- a parent (or group of parents), stating that his or her child is one of a group being discriminated against by a school board; or

- an individual, or his or her parent, stating that he or she has been denied admission to, or dismissed from, a public college, university, or postsecondary vocational or technical school because of race, color, religion, gender, or national origin.

These complaints should be sent to:

U.S. Department of Justice
Civil Rights Division
Educational Opportunities Section
950 Pennsylvania Avenue, NW
Washington, DC 20530
(202) 514-4092
Fax: (202) 514-8337
www.usdoj.gov

If you think you or your child has been discriminated against on the basis of race, color, or national or ethnic origin by a **nonprofit private school** that is exempt from federal income tax, you should contact **IRS** at the following address. IRS can revoke the tax exemption of a private school that has a racially discriminatory policy, which includes discrimination on the bases of color and national or ethnic origin.

Internal Revenue Service
Director, Exempt Organizations Division
1111 Constitution Avenue, NW, 3rd Floor
Washington, DC 20224
(202) 283-2300
Fax: (202) 283-8858
www.irs.gov

If you think your child has been discriminated against because of race, color, or national origin by a vocational, technical, elementary, or secondary school that is privately owned, operated for profit, and not run by a hospital, you should write to:

U.S. Department of Veterans Affairs
Office of Resolution Management
810 Vermont Avenue, NW
Washington, DC 20420
(202) 501-2800
(888) 737-3361
Fax: (202) 501-2885
www.va.gov

The **Department of Veterans Affairs** can act if it pays benefits for any veteran enrolled at the school or otherwise assists that school, even if the person discriminated against is not a veteran.

In addition, federal laws require that public schools provide a free, appropriate public education to children with disabilities. If you believe that your local school system has failed to identify your child's disability, incorrectly identified your child as an individual with a disability, failed to provide an appropriate educational program for your child, failed to carry out the program established for your child, or has unnecessarily separated your child from other children for all or part of the school day, your child may have rights under one or more of the federal laws that govern the education of children with disabilities.

School systems must have formal procedures for identifying, evaluating, and establishing educational programs for children with disabilities. They must also offer a hearing when the parent and school officials disagree whether the program established for a child is appropriate.

Also, if you believe that your child's civil rights were violated because of a failure to follow proper procedures for identifying, evaluating, or placing a student with a disability, or because of a failure to carry out the provisions of your child's educational plan, or were otherwise violated because of discrimination based on disability, you may file a complaint by writing to the **Department of Education, Office for Civil Rights** listed on page 13.

For more information on the Individuals with Disabilities Education Act, write to:

U.S. Department of Education
Assistant Secretary for the Office of Special Education
and Rehabilitative Services
Mary E. Switzer Building
330 C Street, SW
Washington, DC 20202-2500
(202) 205-5507
Fax: (202) 260-0416
TTY: (202) 205-9754
www.ed.gov

Employment

Various federal laws protect you from discrimination in employment on the basis of race, color, sex, religion, national origin, age, or disability. Discrimination by employers with 15 or more employees is prohibited in all aspects of the hiring and employment process: job application, hiring, firing, promoting, training, wage earning, or any other terms, privileges, or conditions of employment provided or imposed by the employer.

If you believe that you have been discriminated against on any of these bases, you should contact the **Equal Employment Opportunity Commission (EEOC)** at:

Equal Employment Opportunity Commission
1801 L Street, NW
Washington, DC 20507
To file charges or reach a field office: (800) 669-4000
Information and publication center: (800) 669-3362
(202) 663-4900
TTY: (202) 663-4494
TTY: (800) 800-3302
www.eeoc.gov

Race and Color

You cannot be denied equal employment opportunity because of your racial group or skin shade, or because you associate with members of some racial group.

National Origin

You cannot be denied equal employment opportunity because of your birthplace, ancestry, or culture, or because you have some intimate association with members of a specific ethnic group, such as by marriage or a shared place of worship.

Likewise, you cannot be denied equal employment opportunity because of your accent or manner of speaking. If an employer believes that an English-proficiency rule is critical for business purposes, he or she must inform you of the rule and the consequences of its violation before applying the rule to you.

Religion

You cannot be denied equal employment opportunity because of your religious practices or beliefs. Religious practices include the exercise of moral and ethical beliefs held with the strength of religious beliefs. If you think your employer has a work requirement (such as a dress code or a work schedule that conflicts with your Sabbath observance) that interferes with your religious practices or beliefs, you must inform them of what reasonable accommodations can be provided to suit your needs. The employer is obligated to try to accommodate your religious practices, unless doing so would create an undue hardship on the operation of the business.

Sex

You cannot be denied equal employment opportunity because of your gender.

▪ *Equal Pay*

It is illegal for an employer to pay you wages at a rate less than the rate of wages paid to employees of the opposite sex for equal work on jobs that require equal skill, effort, and responsibility and are performed under similar working conditions, unless a pay differential is warranted by a seniority system, a merit system, a system that measures earnings by quantity or quality of production, or is based on a factor other than gender.

- *Pregnancy*

You cannot be denied equal employment opportunity because of pregnancy, childbirth, or related medical conditions. Any health insurance provided by an employer must cover expenses for pregnancy-related conditions on the same basis as costs for other medical conditions. Leave for child care should be granted on the same basis as leave granted to employees for other nonmedical reasons, such as non-job-related travel or education, and should be available to both men and women.

Harassment

Hostile or abusive verbal or physical conduct based on race, color, sex, religion, national origin, age, or disability is unlawful if it is sufficiently severe or pervasive to create an intimidating, hostile, or offensive working environment.

Disability

If you have a disability, the Americans with Disabilities Act (ADA) protects you from employment discrimination. The ADA prohibits employers with 15 or more employees from:

- discriminating against you on the basis of physical or mental disability;

- asking you to take medical exams before making a conditional job offer;

- asking you questions about your disability before making a conditional job offer;

- denying you health or other fringe benefits that are provided to other employees; and

- placing you in a job situation that limits your opportunities or status.

If you are able to perform the essential functions of the job with or without reasonable accommodation, the employer has to provide you with reasonable accommodations for your disability, as long as such accommodations do not impose an undue hardship on the operations of the enterprise. An employer may not ask interview questions about your disabilities; inquiries should be about your skills related to the job.

For more information on workplace discrimination against people with disabilities, contact the **Equal Employment Opportunity Commission** listed on page 15.

You may also write to:

U.S. Department of Labor
Office of Disability Employment Policy
200 Constitution Avenue, NW
Washington, DC 20210
(202) 376-6200
TTY: (202) 376-6205
Fax: (202) 376-6219
www.dol.gov/dol/odep/welcome.html

or

A service of the Office of Disability Employment Policy:

Job Accommodation Network
West Virginia University
P.O. Box 6080
Morgantown, WV 26506
Voice/TTY: (800) 526-7234
Fax: (304) 293-5407
BBS: (800) 342-5526
Regional Disability and Business Accommodation Centers
Voice/TTY: (800) 949-4232
www.jan.wvu.edu

Age

If you are 40 years of age or older, it is illegal for an employer with 20 or more employees to:

- discriminate against you in your compensation or terms, conditions, or privileges of employment based on your age;

- classify or segregate you, or limit your activities so you are deprived of job opportunities or adversely affected in employment status;

- discriminate against you in the operation of a seniority system; and

- with certain narrow exceptions, discriminate against you with respect to employee benefit plans, fringe benefits, or pension benefits.

It is also illegal for an employer to indicate an age preference or limitation in notices or advertisements for employment, unless age is a genuine job qualification.

Classifications and preferences based on age have been allowed only in narrow circumstances, generally in jobs involving public safety. To justify unequal treatment, the employer must show that age is a genuine qualification of the job and that there is no other course of action that would achieve his or her goals with a less discriminatory impact.

For more information on age discrimination in the workplace, contact the **Equal Employment Opportunity Commission** on page 15.

Family and Medical Leave

Under the Family and Medical Leave Act (FMLA), you are entitled to a maximum of 12 weeks of unpaid leave during a 12-month period if you work for an employer who has had at least 50 employees during the current or preceding year, you have worked for the employer for at least 12 months, and you have worked at least 1,250 hours in the 12-month period before the leave starts. You must also work at a particular work site where there are at least 50 employees within a 75-mile radius. During the leave, the employer must continue to provide group health benefits on the same basis that such benefits are provided when you are at work. The employer must also restore you to the same or an equivalent position when you are ready to return to work. Leave may be taken for the birth and care of a new child, for placement for adoption or foster care of a child with you, to care for your spouse, child, or a parent who has a serious health condition, or if you must be absent due to your serious health condition. You may elect or the employer may require you to use accrued paid leave during such periods. FMLA leave may also run concurrently with workers' compensation leave or leave covered by short- or long-term disability policies. Employers may not refuse leave, interfere with use of leave, or in any way discriminate against someone who has used leave. **The FMLA protects men and women equally and is enforced by the U.S. Department of Labor.** The federal law does not supersede more generous provisions included in state laws, collective bargaining agreements, or employers' policies. Any less generous provision in such laws, agreements, or policies are, however, superseded by FMLA provisions.

If you feel that your rights under family or medical leave have been violated, you may file a complaint with the local office of the **Wage and Hour Division of the Department of Labor** or you may initiate private action. The address and telephone number of local offices can be found in telephone directories for large cities under **U.S. Department of Labor, Employment Standards Administration, Wage and Hour Division**. If you cannot locate this information, contact the regional office of the Wage and Hour Division listed on page 62 or headquarters listed below.

If you file a complaint with the Wage and Hour Division, the Division will attempt to resolve your complaint administratively by contacting your employer on your behalf. If these efforts fail, the Division may attempt to litigate on your behalf, depending on the facts and circumstances. If you elect private legal action, the Division will not participate. To file a complaint or for more information on FMLA, contact:

U.S. Department of Labor
Employment Standards Administration
Wage and Hour Division
Francis Perkins Building
200 Constitution Avenue, NW
Washington, DC 20210
1-866-4-USA-DOL
TTY: (877) 889-5629
www.dol.gov

Immigration Status

If you are an employee hired after November 6, 1986, your employer must be able to prove that you are legally authorized to work in the United States and will ask you to present documentation showing that you have work authorization. However, an employer cannot single you out to require employment verification because you are of a particular national origin group or you appear not to be a citizen. Neither can an employer require that you be a U.S. citizen, or generally give those who are U.S. citizens a preference in hiring or employment opportunities, unless there are legal or contractual requirements that mandate he or she do so. It is illegal for an employer to discriminate against legal aliens merely because they look like noncitizens or in fact are not citizens or because they have a particular type of work authorization.

Under immigration law, individuals who charge discrimination on the basis of national origin against employers with 4 to 14 employees or on the basis of citizenship status against employers with fewer employees should file a complaint within 180 days of the date of the alleged unfair immigration-related employment practice with the **Office of Special Counsel for Immigration Related Unfair Employment Practices** in the Department of Justice.

For more information about immigrants' employment rights, contact:

U.S. Department of Justice
Office of Special Counsel
for Immigration Related Unfair Employment Practices
950 Pennsylvania Avenue, NW
Washington, DC 20530
(202) 616-5594
Employer hot line: (800) 255-8155
Employee hot line: (800) 255-7688
Fax: (202) 616-5509
www.usdoj.gov/crt/osc

Whatever your characteristic, the **Equal Employment Opportunity Commission (EEOC)** is the agency of the federal government with the mission of protecting you from job discrimination. If you think you have been discriminated against because of race, color, sex, religion, national origin, age, or disability:

- by an **employer** in being hired or tested for a job, in being promoted or fired, in work opportunities or conditions, in pay or benefits, or in apprenticeship or training programs;

- by a **labor union** in its apprenticeship or training programs, hiring hall procedures, or membership requirements; or

- by an **employment agency**, including state employment services, in its job testing, referrals, or fees;

write or phone the nearest office of **EEOC** listed on page 66. The office will give you instructions and forms for filing a charge.

Charges must be filed within 180 or 300 days of the discriminatory act. In states or localities without an antidiscrimination law, charges must be filed with EEOC within 180 days of the discriminatory act. In states or localities where there is an antidiscrimination law and an agency authorized to grant or seek relief, charges must be filed with EEOC within 300 days of the discriminatory act. The local EEOC office can tell you what procedures and time limits apply to your charge.

Although EEOC prefers that its forms be used, it will accept a complaint filed in the form of a letter containing your name and address and that of the employer, union, or employment office you think has discriminated. You must date the letter and briefly explain what the discriminatory act was and when it occurred.

Contact one of the district offices of EEOC listed on page 66 or EEOC headquarters:

Equal Employment Opportunity Commission
1801 L Street, NW
Washington, DC 20507
To file charges or reach a field office: (800) 669-4000
Information and publication center: (800) 669-3362
(202) 663-4900
TTY: (202) 663-4494
TTY: (800) 669-6820
www.eeoc.gov

If EEOC does not act within 180 days of the filing of your complaint, you may request a right-to-sue letter from EEOC and file a private lawsuit in federal district court. You have only 90 days to file a lawsuit after you receive a right-to-sue letter. If the discrimination complaint deals with equal pay, you do not have to file a charge with EEOC before filing a lawsuit. The Department of Justice (DOJ) is responsible for employment discrimination litigation involving state and local governments. The EEOC will refer requests for right-to-sue letters involving public employers to DOJ, which will issue the letter.

A presidential order (Executive Order 11,246) also forbids employment discrimination on the basis of race, color, national origin, sex, or religion by companies that hold contracts or subcontracts with the federal government and by firms working on construction projects that receive federal funds. In addition, the Rehabilitation Act of 1973, as amended, forbids employment discrimination on the basis of disability by companies that hold contracts or subcontracts with the federal government. Employers holding contracts or subcontracts with the federal government are also barred from discriminating against qualified disabled veterans and veterans of the Vietnam era. If you think an employer who has discriminated against you holds a contract with a federal agency, contact the **Office of Federal Contract Compliance Programs (OFCCP), Department of Labor** listed below, or one of the OFCCP regional offices listed on page 61.

U.S. Department of Labor
Employment Standards Administration
Office of Federal Contract Compliance Programs
200 Constitution Avenue, NW, Room C3310
Washington, DC 20210
1-866-4-USA-DOL
Fax: (877) 889-5627
www.dol.gov

Complaints must be filed within 180 days of the date of the alleged discrimination, unless an OFCCP director extends it for a good reason. If you are disabled or a Vietnam era veteran, you must file within 300 days, unless filing is extended for good cause. If your complaint is an individual complaint of discrimination against an employer, it will probably be referred to EEOC. If it is one of systemic discrimination or if there are several complaints, or if many other persons are also affected by a pattern and practice of discrimination, the Labor Department will generally take the lead in processing the complaint.

OFCCP also has an ombudsperson who receives and investigates complaints made by individuals alleging abuse by OFCCP staff in the processing of discrimination complaints or conduct of compliance reviews. The ombudsperson can be reached by telephone on **(303) 844-1210** or by fax at **(303) 844-1213**.

If you are a federal employee, or an applicant for federal employment, and think you have been discriminated against, contact the equal employment director of the agency involved within 45 days of the alleged discrimination. That person will provide information about filing a complaint. If the agency rules against you, you should ask the equal employment opportunity director what appeal rights you have and what the time limits are for filing an appeal.

If your complaint concerns an action that may be appealed to the **Merit Systems Protection Board (MSPB)**, such as being fired, you must include the discrimination issues as part of your appeal to MSPB, which must be filed within 30 calendar days of the effective date of the action, or within 30 calendar days after the date of receipt of the agency's decision whichever is later, or you must raise these issues separately in your agency's EEO administrative process. The EEO administrative process differs when a personnel action can be appealed to MSPB and when it cannot; therefore, you must request your EEO counselor to provide you with information about the differences. The MSPB complaint forms can be obtained from your agency, the regional office of the Merit Systems Protection Board listed on page 75, or the Office of the Clerk of MSPB by writing to:

U.S. Merit Systems Protection Board
Clerk of the Board
1615 M Street, NW
Washington, DC 20419
(202) 653-7200
(800) 209-8960
TTY: (202) 653-8896
Fax: (202) 653-7130
www.mspb.gov

If you are a federal employee entitled to use a negotiated grievance procedure that covers the alleged discrimination, you may elect to file a grievance pursuant to the negotiated procedure in your collective bargaining agreement or to file an EEO complaint, but not both.

It is a prohibited personnel practice to discriminate against a federal employee or an applicant for federal employment on the basis of race, color, national origin, religion, sex, age, disability, marital status, or political affiliation. Though the **Office of Special Counsel** generally defers to the agency's EEO program, you may file a discrimination complaint with:

U.S. Office of Special Counsel
Complaints Examining Unit
1730 M Street, NW, Suite 218
Washington, DC 20036-4505
Public Information: (202) 653-7984
(202) 254-3670
(800) 872-9855
TTY: (800) 877-8339
www.osc.gov

If you are an employee of a **state or local government**, an employment discrimination complaint on the basis of race, color, national origin, religion, sex, disability, or age may be filed with EEOC. EEOC may defer resolution of your complaint to the state or local fair employment practices agency depending on the terms of a particular work-sharing agreement. The **Employment Litigation Section of the Civil Rights Division of the Department of Justice** sues state and local government employers who discriminate in employment on the grounds of race, national origin, sex, or religion. EEOC will refer such cases and disability cases in which it appears that discrimination has occurred to the Department of Justice for litigation consideration, if conciliation has failed. If you think you have been discriminated against by a state or local government and wish to file a charge, write to the **Equal Employment Opportunity Commission** (listed on page 15).

EEOC may sue the state or local government in cases involving age discrimination and sex-based pay discrimination.

If you think you have been discriminated against by a state employment service (although its actions are also covered by EEOC), unemployment benefits office, or by Comprehensive Employment and Training Act (CETA) job-training or public service employment programs, write to the appropriate regional office of the **Department of Labor**. For addresses, see page 61. If you think you have been discriminated against by an apprenticeship program registered with the Department of Labor or a state apprenticeship agency, write to:

U.S. Department of Labor
Employment and Training Administration
Bureau of Apprenticeship and Training
200 Constitution Avenue, NW, Room N-4649
Washington, DC 20210
(202) 219-5921
TTY: 219-6325
Fax: (202) 693-3900
www.doleta.gov

If you think you have been discriminated against by a job-training center that receives federal assistance, write to the appropriate federal agency. For example, the Department of Veterans Affairs can act if it pays benefits for any veteran enrolled at the school, or otherwise assists the school, even if the person discriminated against is not a veteran.

If you think you have been discriminated against by a criminal justice agency that is receiving federal funds from the **Office of Justice Programs,** you may write to:

U.S. Department of Justice
Office of Justice Programs
Office for Civil Rights
810 7th Street, NW
Washington, DC 20531
(202) 307-0690
TTY: (202) 307-2027
Fax: (202) 616-9865

Complaints of employment discrimination on the basis of disability by law enforcement agencies that received Department of Justice funds may also be sent to:

U.S. Department of Justice
Civil Rights Division
Disability Rights Section
950 Pennsylvania Avenue, NW
Washington, DC 20530
(202) 307-2227
(800) 514-0301
TTY: (800) 514-0383
Fax: (202) 307-1198
www.usdoj.gov/crt/ada

Numerous other federal agencies, such as the Department of Agriculture, the Federal Communications Commission, the Treasury Department, the Securities and Exchange Commission, and the Environmental Protection Agency, enforce statutes that contain prohibitions against discrimination by particular groups of employers. In almost all cases, EEOC also has jurisdiction. An individual's rights and remedies may differ from agency to agency. It may be to your advantage to contact all involved agencies you think may enforce laws covering your situation so that you can make an informed decision as to the most appropriate agency with which to file a complaint.

EEOC is responsible for coordinating federal enforcement of laws against employment discrimination. In addition, its Office of Equal Employment Opportunity works with all federal agencies in developing more effective procedures and uniform standards for handling complaints and ensuring compliance with employment discrimination laws. If you believe a complaint filed with another agency has not been properly handled, you should write to:

Equal Employment Opportunity Commission
Office of Equal Employment Opportunity
1801 L Street, NW, Room 9029
Washington, DC 20507
(202) 663-4900
Fax: (202) 663-7003
www.eeoc.gov

Information on all EEOC-enforced laws may be obtained by calling **toll-free 1-800-669-EEOC**. EEOC's **toll-free TTY number is (800) 800-3302**. For other information, call the Office of Equal Opportunity at **(202) 663-4395 (voice)** or **(202) 663-4399 (TTY)** or write to:

Equal Employment Opportunity Commission
Office of Communications and Legislative Affairs
1801 L Street, NW
Washington, DC 20507
(202) 663-4900
TTY: (202) 663-4494
Fax: (202) 663-4912
www.eeoc.gov

Hate Crimes/Campus Anti-Semitism

Hate crimes are criminal offenses committed against persons, property, or society motivated by prejudice or bias against an individual's or group's race, religion, disability, sexual orientation or national origin.

For instance, serious incidents of campus anti-Semitism have occurred on campuses around the nation, including threats of violence that may be conveyed through swastikas painted on walls, destruction of property, and physical and verbal assaults. Federal law prohibits the use of force or threat of force to interfere with a person engaging in various federally protected activities, including attending a public college or university, on the basis of race, color, religion, or national origin.

If you think you have been the victim of a hate crime, contact:

U.S. Department of Justice
Civil Rights Division
Criminal Section
950 Pennsylvania Avenue, NW
Washington, DC 20530
(202) 514-3204
Fax: (202) 514-8336

You may also report such crimes to your area Federal Bureau of Investigations (FBI).

Housing

Discrimination in the sale or rental of housing on the basis of race, color, national origin, religion, sex, disability, or family status (having children) is illegal. On such a basis, it is illegal to:

- refuse to rent or sell housing;

- refuse to negotiate for housing;

- make housing unavailable;

- deny housing;

- set different terms, conditions, or privileges for the sale or rental of a dwelling, or provide different services or facilities in connection with the sale or rental;

- falsely deny that housing is available for inspection, sale, or rental;

- engage in blockbusting practices by persuading owners to sell or rent by telling them that minorities are moving into a neighborhood;

- deny anyone access to or membership in a facility or service related to the sale or rental of housing, such as membership in multiple listing services or real estate brokers' organizations;

- make, print, or publish, or cause to be made, printed, or published any notice, statement, or advertisement indicating any preference, limitation, or discrimination with respect to the sale or rental of a dwelling;

- discriminate in the making or purchasing of loans or providing other financial services for a dwelling, including making available property insurance;

- discriminate in the appraising of residential property; or

- refuse to permit reasonable alterations to make a dwelling accessible for disabled tenants, or to provide reasonable accommodations for equal opportunity to enjoy the dwelling.

If you think you have been discriminated against:

- in trying to buy or rent a house or apartment;

- in getting a housing loan (see also the section on credit);

- in seeking real estate broker services;

or if you wish to complain about advertisements that say housing is available only to persons of a certain race, color, national origin, sex, or religion, you may file a complaint with the nearest **Fair Housing Enforcement Center of the Department of Housing and Urban Development (HUD)** listed on page 58 or with:

U.S. Department of Housing and Urban Development
Office of Fair Housing and Equal Opportunity
451 Seventh Street, SW, Room 5204
Washington, DC 20410-2000
(202) 619-8041
Hot line: (800) 669-9777, (202) 708-0836
TTY: (800) 927-9275
Fax: (202) 708-1425
www.hud.gov

For more information about how to file a complaint or to obtain forms, call the Fair Housing Clearinghouse at **(800) 343-3442**.

You may file suit, at your expense, in federal district court or state court. You may bring suit even after filing a complaint, if you have not signed a conciliation agreement and an administrative law judge has not started a hearing. You must file suit within 2 years of the alleged discriminatory action.

Finally, you may file a complaint with the U.S. Department of Justice, which may step in if a pattern or practice of discrimination appears to exist, or if the denial of rights to a group of persons raises an important public issue. Send the complaint to:

U.S. Department of Justice
Civil Rights Division
Housing and Civil Enforcement Section
950 Pennsylvania Avenue, NW
Washington, DC 20530
(202) 514-4713
Fax: (202) 514-1116
www.usdoj.gov

If you think you have been discriminated against in seeking **real estate broker services**, where such services include credit referral, you should also send a complaint to:

Federal Trade Commission
Bureau of Consumer Protection
FTC Building
600 Pennsylvania Avenue, NW
Washington, DC 20580
(202) 326-2222
TTY: (202) 326-2050
Fax: (202) 326-2050
www.ftc.gov

Neither HUD nor the Justice Department has authority to act in some instances of discrimination, such as those that occur in the sale or rental of a single-family home by a private individual who owns three or fewer such units and does not advertise or use a broker, or in the rental of a room or apartment in a dwelling containing four or fewer units, if the owner lives in one of them.

Law Enforcement

Federal criminal civil rights law prohibits law enforcement agents from conspiring to interfere with federally protected rights, depriving rights under color of law, or using or conspiring to use force, or threat of force, to interfere with the free exercise of your civil rights.

To report criminal activities that constitute violations of civil rights, contact:

U.S. Department of Justice
Civil Rights Division
Criminal Section, PHB
950 Pennsylvania Avenue, NW
Washington, DC 20530
(202) 514-3204
Fax: (202) 514-8336
www.usdoj.gov

If you have a complaint of police brutality or the abuse of your rights by the police or other public officials, contact the nearest office of the **Federal Bureau of Investigation (FBI)**, listed in the front of your telephone directory under "police," or write to the **Department of Justice** at the address above.

An individual who believes that a law enforcement agency receiving Department of Justice assistance, such as a police or sheriff's department, jail, state police, or corrections system, is discriminating on the basis of race, color, national origin, religion, sex, or age may file a complaint with:

29

U.S. Department of Justice
Civil Rights Division
Coordination and Review Section
950 Pennsylvania Avenue, NW
Washington, DC 20530
(202) 307-2222
TTY: (202) 307-2678
Fax: (202) 307-0595
www.usdoj.gov/crt/cor/index.htm

or

U.S. Department of Justice
Office of Justice Programs
Office for Civil Rights
810 Seventh Street, NW, Room 8124
Washington, DC 20531
(202) 307-0690
TTY: (202) 307-2027
Fax: (202) 616-9865
www.ojp.usdoj.gov/ocr

Complaints of discrimination on the basis of disability by law enforcement agencies may also be sent to:

U.S. Department of Justice
Civil Rights Division
Disability Rights Section
950 Pennsylvania Avenue, NW
Washington, DC 20530
(202) 307-2227
(800) 514-0301
TTY: (800) 514-0383
Fax: (202) 307-1198

Prisoners

The constitutional rights of inmates are very limited. Prisoners' rights that are protected are:

- a right to be free from cruel and unusual punishment, which is usually construed to mean the infliction of unnecessary and unrestricted pain; and

- a right to exercise religious beliefs. Prisoners must be allowed the opportunity to pray and to meet with other inmates to worship within a

30

group. Even individuals in disciplinary detention are entitled to pray and read religious texts.

Also, the Equal Protection Clause of the 14th Amendment to the Constitution requires that the conditions of women's prisons be equal to the conditions under which male prisoners are held, and vice versa.

If you are confined to a **Federal Bureau of Prisons** institution and believe you have been discriminated against by the institution, you should file a formal written complaint at the institution within **20 calendar days** of the incident. Extensions of time will be granted where there is a valid reason for the delay. You should follow the internal grievance procedure unless you think that your complaint is such that you might be adversely affected if the nature of the complaint became known within the institution, in which case you may file the complaint with the appropriate Regional Director of the Bureau of Prisons (for addresses, see page 51). Your complaint should include an explanation of why you have chosen to file with the Regional Director. If the complaint alleges that your health or welfare is immediately threatened, the warden must respond through the regional office within 48 hours of receiving the complaint.

If you are confined to a **non-federal institution** and want to file a complaint about conditions or practices of the institution, follow the internal grievance procedure of the institution. In some prison systems it is necessary to file an institutional grievance before filing suit in federal court.

Under the Civil Rights of Institutionalized Persons Act, the Attorney General is authorized to file suit on behalf of inmates at a given institution to redress systematic deprivations of inmates' constitutional rights. To file a complaint with the Attorney General, write to:

U.S. Department of Justice
Civil Rights Division
Special Litigation Section
950 Pennsylvania Avenue, NW
Washington, DC 20530
(202) 514-6255
(877) 218-5228
Fax: (202) 514-0212
www.usdoj.gov/crt/split/index.html

Under the Americans with Disabilities Act (ADA), prisoners with disabilities, particularly prisoners with HIV, may have a right to participate in various services, programs, and activities. Complaints of discrimination under the ADA should be filed with the **Department of Justice** (for address, see page 25) within **180 days** of the alleged discriminatory act.

Federally Assisted Programs

Discrimination on the basis of race, color, national origin, age, or disability in federally assisted programs is prohibited. This prohibition applies to recipients of federal assistance and subrecipients. Discrimination on the basis of sex or religion is also prohibited in some federally assisted programs. Discrimination on the basis of sex is prohibited in all federally assisted education programs.

In addition, recipients of federal funds are required to provide linguistic accessibility to individuals with limited English proficiency (LEP), such as translation services and written notice informing them of their rights.

Laws barring discrimination because of race, color, national origin, or disability in federally assisted programs cover benefits and services provided by the program. As a result, recipients of federal assistance may not discriminate to:

- deny an individual service, aid, or benefits;

- provide only inferior or discriminatory service, aid, or benefits;

- subject an individual to segregation or different treatment in relation to aid, service, or benefits;

- restrict or discourage individuals in their access to and usage of facilities;

- treat an individual differently in regard to eligibility for programs or services;

- use criteria that would impair accomplishment of the program's objectives or that would subject individuals to discrimination; or

- deny an individual access to any program or activity that is conducted in a facility constructed wholly or partly with federal funds.

Laws barring discrimination in federally assisted programs usually do not cover employment by the program, unless: (1) a main purpose of the operation is to provide employment; (2) discrimination in employment could cause discrimination in benefits or services; or (3) an allegation of disability discrimination is made.

In the event that employment is covered, you should file such a complaint with the federal agency funding the program. Also, job discrimination is covered by other laws, and complaints should also be filed as described in the employment section of this publication. See page 15.

Laws barring discrimination in federally assisted programs are normally enforced by the agency that provides the assistance. If a recipient of federal funds is found to be discriminating and refuses to come into compliance with the law, the federal agency may terminate the funding to that recipient or refer the case to the Department of Justice for possible litigation.

Complaints alleging discrimination in federally assisted programs should generally be filed with the appropriate federal agency within 180 days of the alleged discriminatory act. However, some agencies allow more time to file a complaint, while others allow as few as 90 days. You should check with the appropriate agency as quickly as possible if you believe you have been discriminated against. If you do not know which federal agency funds the program, but you believe it probably receives federal assistance, you may file with the **Coordination and Review Section of the Department of Justice** (see page 41). That office will refer your complaint to the appropriate federal agency.

Information on where to file complaints about federally assisted education, employment, housing, and law enforcement programs is contained in other sections of chapter 3. Programs in agriculture, health and welfare, recreation, transportation, environmental control, and other fields are covered in this section.

Department of Agriculture

The Department of Agriculture handles complaints alleging discrimination in **agricultural and rural programs**. Some complaints that should be filed with the Department of Agriculture are:

- discrimination in **Extension Programs**, such as in 4-H club participation;

- discrimination in the **Food Stamp Program**, such as discrimination in distribution of food stamp benefits;

- discrimination in the **Rural Rental Housing Program,** such as biased eviction from a rural rental housing (apartment-style) complex because of lease violations; and

- discrimination in **Rural Utility Programs**, such as in providing telephone, electric, or waste water facilities.

All of these programs are covered by laws or regulations prohibiting discrimination based on race, national origin, color, age, or disability. Housing programs are also covered by laws or regulations that prohibit discrimination based on marital/family status and religion.

If you believe you have been discriminated against by one of the above programs or by any other program that receives assistance from the Department of Agriculture, send your complaint to:

33

U.S. Department of Agriculture
Director, Office of Adjudication and Compliance
1400 Independence Avenue, SW
Washington, DC 20250-9410(202) 260-1026
TDD: (202) 401-0216
(866) 632-9992
Fax: (202) 690-5686
www.usda.gov/cr

Department of Energy

To conserve needed energy and aid those persons least able to afford higher utility costs, the **Department of Energy's** weatherization assistance program makes funds available to states, local governments, community action agencies, and, in certain instances, Native American tribal organizations to insulate the dwellings of low-income persons, especially the elderly and disabled. All low-income households are eligible to receive this assistance, which includes the making of furnace efficiency modifications and the installation of weatherization materials such as ceiling insulation, caulking, weather stripping, and storm windows.

If you think you have been discriminated against by a state or local government or by a community action agency in trying to get assistance under the weatherization program, write to:

U.S. Department of Energy
Office of Civil Rights
1000 Independence Avenue, SW, Room 5B168
Washington, DC 20585
(202) 586-2218
(800) 424-9246
Fax: (202) 586-0888
www.doe.gov

Environmental Protection Agency

The **Environmental Protection Agency** provides financial assistance to state and local governments, tribal governments, and local education programs (this means any educational program or activity, not only those conducted by a formal educational institution) that deal, among others, with:

- pollution control and prevention;

- the development of municipal wastewater treatment facilities;

- the removal of asbestos from schools; or

- hazardous waste site identification, health risk assessment, and cleanup.

Allegations that residents of predominantly minority and low-income communities bear a disproportionate share of environmentally related health risks are investigated by the agency's external compliance program, which is managed in collaboration with the agency's **Office of Environmental Justice**.

If you think that you have been discriminated against in programs funded by the EPA write to:

U.S. Environmental Protection Agency
Office of Civil Rights
1200 Pennsylvania Avenue, NW, Room 2540
Washington, DC 20460
(202) 564-7272
(800) 424-9346
TTY: (202) 260-4565
Fax: (202) 501-1836
www.epa.gov

Department of Health and Human Services

Many institutions and people receive funding from the **Department of Health and Human Services (HHS)**. Among them are:

- hospitals;

- nursing homes and extended care facilities;

- family health centers and clinics;

- alcohol and drug treatment centers;

- community mental health centers;

- physicians and other health professionals in private practice with patients assisted by Medicaid;

- state agencies responsible for administering health care;

- state and local public assistance agencies;

- day care centers;

- adoption agencies;

- foster care homes;

- senior citizen centers; and

- nutrition programs.

If you think you have been discriminated against by an entity that receives funds from **HHS,** send the complaint to a Regional Manager of the Office for Civil Rights listed on page 56 or to:

listed on page 56

U.S. Department of Health and Human Services
Director, Office for Civil Rights
200 Independence Avenue, SW, Room 509F
Washington, DC 20201
(202) 619-0403
Voice hot line: (202) 863-0100
TTY: (202) 863-0101
Voice toll-free: (800) 368-1019
TTY toll-free: (800) 537-7697
Fax: (202) 619-3818
www.hhs.gov/ocr

Department of the Interior

The **Department of the Interior** provides funding for natural resource, recreation, and wildlife programs. Through its **National Park Service**, the Department provides funds to:

- states for park acquisition and outdoor public recreation projects;

- states to expand the National Register of Historic Places and for the identification, evaluation, and protection of historic properties;

- the National Trust for Historic Preservation for its activities; and

- eligible cities and counties for the rehabilitation of recreation areas and facilities, demonstration of innovative approaches to park management and recreation opportunities, and for recreation planning.

If you think that you have, or your community has been discriminated against in the receipt of any of these National Park Service funds, contact:

U.S. Department of the Interior
National Park Service
Office of Equal Opportunity
1201 I Street, NW
Washington, DC 20005
(202) 354-1852
Fax: (202) 321-1449
www.doi.gov

The **Fish and Wildlife Service** provides federal financial assistance for:

- projects aimed at restoring and managing the sport fish population or improving sport fishing; and

- state fish and wildlife agencies to restore or manage wildlife populations and for hunter-safety programs.

If you think you have, or your community has been discriminated against in Fish and Wildlife Service programs, write to:

U.S. Department of the Interior
Fish and Wildlife Programs
Federally Assisted and Conducted Programs
Webb Building
4040 North Fairfax Drive, Room 300
Arlington, VA 22203
(703) 358-1724
TTY: (703) 358-2549
Fax: (703) 358-2030

Complaints regarding all other programs funded by the Department of the Interior should be sent to:

U.S. Department of the Interior
Office of Equal Opportunity
Federal Financial Assistance Programs
Interior Building
1849 C Street, NW, Room MS5214
Washington, DC 20240
(202) 208-5694
TTY: (202) 208-5998
Fax: (202) 208-6112

Department of Transportation

Programs funded by the **Department of Transportation (DOT)** are prohibited from discriminating on the bases of race, color, national origin, sex, disability, age, and low-income status. If you believe that an entity which receives funds from DOT, or an entity involved in transportation under the Americans with Disabilities Act, is discriminating in providing or denying a service, write to:

U.S. Department of Transportation
Departmental Office of Civil Rights
1200 New Jersey Avenue, SE
Room W35-208
Washington, DC 20590
(202) 366-4648
TTY: (202) 366-5273
Fax: (202) 366-9371
www.dot.gov/ost/docr

You may also write to the appropriate operating administration's Office of Civil Rights listed below.

For highways, curb cuts, parking for people with disabilities, write to:

Federal Highway Administration
Office of Civil Rights
1200 New Jersey Avenue, SE
Room ES-101
Washington, DC 20590
(202) 366-0693
TTY: (202) 366-5751
Fax: (202) 366-1599
www.dot.gov

For railroads and AMTRAK, write to:

Federal Railroad Administration
Office of Civil Rights, ROA-10
1200 New Jersey Avenue, SE
Washington, DC 20590
(202) 493-6010
TTY: (202) 493-6488
Fax: (202) 493-6009

For public surface transportation such as buses, paratransit vehicles, and subways, write to:

Federal Transit Administration
Office of Civil Rights
1200 New Jersey Avenue, SE, Stop3/E54-427
Washington, DC 20590
(202) 366-4018
TDD: (202) 366-0153
TTY: (800) 877-8339
Fax: 202-366-3475
www.fta.dot.gov/index.html

For airline disputes, write to:

Aviation Consumer Protection Division
Office of Aviation Enforcement Proceedings, C-75
1200 New Jersey Avenue, SW
Washington, DC 20590
(202) 366-2220
TTY: (202) 366-0511
www.airconsumer.ost.dot.gov

For businesses serving the public on airport property, write to:

Federal Aviation Administration
Assistant Administrator for Civil Rights, ACR-1
800 Independence Avenue, SW, Room 1030
Washington, DC 20591
(202) 267-3254
Fax: (202) 267-5565
www.dot.gov

For driver's licensing and motor vehicle bureaus, write to:

National Highway Traffic Safety Administration
Office of Civil Rights, NOA-20
1200 New Jersey Avenue, SE, Room W43-324
Washington, DC 20590
(202) 366-6795
TTY: (800) 877-0996
Fax: (202) 366-3475
www.dot.gov

For ports, ships, and their certification and licensing, write to:

U.S. Coast Guard
Office of Civil Rights, G-H
2100 Second Street, SW, Room 2400
Washington, DC 20593
(202) 267-1562
Fax: (202) 267-4282
www.uscg.mil

If you think you have been discriminated against by a program operated under a community development grant, write to the appropriate area office of the **Department of Housing and Urban Development** listed in your telephone book. You may also call one of the telephone numbers listed on page 28.

If you think you have been discriminated against by the **National Guard**, the **Civilian Health and Medical Programs of the Uniformed Services (CHAMPUS)**, or by another defense program, such as a program of the **U.S. Army Corps of Engineers** or of the **Defense Civil Preparedness Agency**, write to:

U.S. Department of Defense
Deputy Assistant Secretary of Defense, Equal Opportunity
4000 Defense, The Pentagon, Room 3A272
Washington, DC 20301-4000
(703) 693-0105
Fax: (703) 697-7534
www.dtic.mil

If you think you have been discriminated against by any program funded or assisted by the **Department of Commerce**, write to:

U.S. Department of Commerce
Office of Civil Rights
Herbert C. Hoover Building
14th Street and Constitution Avenue, NW, Room 6012
Washington, DC 20230
(202) 482-5691
TTY: (202) 482-5691
TTY: (800) 877-8339
Fax: (202) 482-5375
www.osec.doc.gov/ocr

If you think you have been discriminated against by a company that receives or dispenses **Small Business Administration** funds, write to:

U.S. Small Business Administration
Equal Employment Opportunity and Civil Rights Compliance
409 Third Street, SW, Suite 4600
Washington, DC 20416
(202) 205-6750
(800) 827-5722
TTY: (202) 205-7150
Fax: (202) 205-7580
www.sba.gov

Direct discrimination by a federal agency in awarding grants to community organizations, governments, or others is not necessarily barred by federal statutes. However, it is prohibited by the U.S. Constitution. Complaints should be filed with the agency responsible for the discriminatory act; if that agency does not act, you may have to file a lawsuit to protect your rights.

The Coordination and Review Section of the Civil Rights Division of the Department of Justice serves as the coordinator of enforcement by federal agencies of all statutes that prohibit discrimination in programs that receive federal financial assistance. If you think you have been discriminated against by an agency that receives federal assistance and you don't know which agency to contact, write to the Coordination and Review Section at the address below:

U.S. Department of Justice
Civil Rights Division
Coordination and Review Section
950 Pennsylvania Avenue, NW
Washington, DC 20530
(202) 307-2222
TTY: (202) 307-2678
Fax: (202) 307-0595
www.usdoj.gov/crt/cor/index.htm

Public Accommodations and Facilities

Federal law prohibits privately owned facilities that offer food, lodging, gasoline or entertainment to the public from discriminating on the basis of race, color, religion, or national origin. If you think that you have been discriminated against in using such a facility, you may file a complaint with the Civil Rights Division of the Department of Justice, or with the United States attorney in your area. You may also file suit in the U.S. district court.

In addition, the Americans with Disabilities Act prohibits discrimination on the basis of disability in a wide range of places of public accommodation, including facilities that offer lodging, food, entertainment, sales or rental services, health care and other professional services, or recreation. If you feel that a place of public accommodation has discriminated against you on the basis of your disability, you should follow the procedures addressed on page 4.

There are also state laws that broadly prohibit discrimination on the bases of race, color, religion, national origin, and disability in places of public accommodation. To determine whether your state has such a law, you should contact your state or local human rights agency, or your state attorney general's office.

Public facilities such as courthouses, jails, hospitals, parks, and other facilities owned and operated by state and local government entities cannot discriminate in their services because of race, color, religion, national origin, or disability. If you think a public facility has discriminated against you because of race, color, religion, or national origin, you may file suit in the U.S. district court or file a complaint with the nearest U.S. Attorney's Office (see page 79).

People with disabilities cannot be discriminated against or excluded from services, programs, or activities offered by state or local governments. All public transportation systems must be accessible to people with disabilities, regardless of whether the system receives federal financial assistance.

State and local governments must eliminate any eligibility criteria for participation in programs, activities, and services that screen out or tend to screen out persons with disabilities, unless the government can establish that the requirements are necessary for the provision of the service, program, or activity. In addition, public facilities must ensure that individuals with disabilities are not excluded from services, programs, or activities because buildings are inaccessible.

State and local agencies that provide emergency telephone services must provide "direct access" to individuals who rely on TTY or computer modems for telephone communication. Companies offering telephone services to the general public must offer telephone relay services to individuals who use TTYs or similar devices.

Intrastate complaints should be filed with that state. Interstate complaints should be filed with the Federal Communications Commission.

Discrimination complaints about public facilities (other than Architectural Barriers Act complaints) should be sent to:

- the federal agency that provides funding to the facility subject to the complaint;

- the federal agency designated to investigate complaints; or

- the Department of Justice.

Complaints may always be filed with the Civil Rights Division of the Department of Justice, which will refer your complaint to the appropriate agency.

Complaints regarding new construction of, or alterations to buildings or facilities funded by the federal government and subject to the Architectural Barriers Act of 1968 should be sent to:

Architectural and Transportation Barriers Compliance Board
Office of Compliance and Enforcement
1331 F Street, NW, Suite 1000
Washington, DC 20004-1111
(202) 272-0800
(800) 872-2253
TTY: (202) 272-0082
TTY: (800) 993-2822
Fax: (202) 272-0081
www.access-board.gov

The **Disability Rights Section** of the Civil Rights Division of the U.S. Department of Justice handles complaints of discrimination based on disability in places of public accommodation, including all hotels, restaurants, retail stores, theaters, health care facilities, convention centers, parks, and places of recreation. To file a complaint of discrimination based on disability, call **(800) 514-0301** and send your complaint to:

U.S. Department of Justice
Civil Rights Division
Disability Rights Section
950 Pennsylvania Avenue, NW
Washington, DC 20530
(202) 307-2227
TTY: (800) 514-0383
Fax: (202) 307-1198
www.usdoj.gov

If the Disability Rights Section of the Civil Rights Division believes that there is a pattern or practice of discrimination, or the complaint raises an issue of general public importance, it may attempt to negotiate a settlement of the matter, or bring an action in U.S. district court. Any such action would be taken on behalf of the United States. You also have the option of filing your own lawsuit in U.S. district court.

Voting

Federal laws prohibit discrimination in voting practices on the basis of race, color, previous condition of servitude, sex, disability, being a member of a language minority, or age if you are 18 years of age or older. The prohibition because of race or color is directed against the United States, state and local governments, and private organizations such as political parties. Your right to vote in general interest elections cannot be restricted by classifications on grounds other than residence, age, and citizenship, unless the classification serves a compelling state interest. General interest elections involve the voting on important governmental functions, such as imposition of property or sales taxes, maintenance of streets, operation of schools (including school board elections), and providing of sanitation, health, or welfare services.

The imposition by a state or voting district of a voting qualification, a prerequisite for registration or voting, or some other standard, practice, or procedure based on race, color, or membership in a language minority group that results in a denial of your right to vote or to participate in the processes leading to a nomination or election is forbidden by federal laws. It is also forbidden to have as a prerequisite for voting that you demonstrate the ability to read, write, understand, or interpret any matter, demonstrate any educational achievement or knowledge of any particular subject, or possess good moral character. If you cannot read or write, voting officials are required to permit you to receive assistance from a person of your choice so that you can vote.

States may require you to provide some information, including identification information such as race, in order to determine your eligibility to vote and prevent voter fraud. A state may take away your right to vote if you are a convicted felon, but only as long as the purpose of the rule is not to disenfranchise you as a member of a minority group.

The federal government requires that a voter registration application be provided simultaneously with an application for, or renewal of, a driver's license or other personal identification document issued by a state motor vehicle authority. States are also required to provide registration materials by mail and in all public libraries, public schools, unemployment offices, Armed Forces recruitment offices, state offices that provide public assistance, and state-funded programs primarily engaged in providing services to those with disabilities.

A federal write-in absentee ballot is provided to overseas citizens who do not receive a regular ballot from a state or territory if the request was received at least 30 days before the election.

If you are a member of a language minority and unable to participate effectively in English language elections, your state or voting district must provide you with registration and voting notices, forms, instructions, assistance, and other materials and information relating to the electoral process, including ballots, in English and in your language if your county has been determined to satisfy criteria contained in the minority language provisions of the Voting Rights Act.

As a safeguard against discrimination, jurisdictions covered under the special provisions of the Voting Rights Act must seek approval from either the Attorney General or the U.S. District Court for the District of Columbia before making changes in voting practices or procedures. Also, the Attorney General is authorized to request that federal observers be sent to such jurisdictions to monitor polling place activities on Election Day.

If you think you were discriminated against when you tried to vote or register to vote, immediately complain to local voting officials, and contact the nearest **United States Attorney's Office** (see page 79) or write to the **Voting Section of the Civil Rights Division of the Department of Justice** at the address below. You should also complain if you were discriminated against in campaigning for office, or when you took part in a political meeting, signed up other voters, or served as an election official or poll watcher, or if you think a change in local voting laws has a discriminatory purpose or effect.

The Voting Section also safeguards the right to vote of the disabled and illiterate persons, overseas citizens, persons who change their residence shortly before a presidential election, and persons 18 or older discriminated against because of their age. The U.S. Attorney General may bring a civil action in federal district court to enforce your right to vote. As a private individual, you may also bring a civil action to remedy discriminatory behavior.

To file a voting complaint with the **Department of Justice**, write to:

U.S. Department of Justice
Civil Rights Division
Voting Rights Section
950 Pennsylvania Avenue, NW
Washington, DC 20530
(202) 514-4609
Fax: (202) 307-3961
TTY: (202) 514-0716
www.usdoj.gov/crt/crt-home.html

4. Special Circumstances

Immigration-Related Employment Discrimination

The Constitution protects, to some extent, people in the United States who are not citizens from arbitrary denial of rights.

Discrimination in employment, education, and social services are some areas of concern to noncitizens.

If you are discriminated against in employment based on citizenship or immigration status, you may file a complaint at the **Office of Special Counsel for Immigration Related Unfair Employment Practices** of the Department of Justice within 180 days of the discriminatory action if you are a:

- legal permanent resident who filed for citizenship within 6 months of becoming eligible;

- legal temporary resident;

- refugee; or

- asylee.

You are also protected against national origin discrimination, a refusal to accept proper identity papers or a work authorization or both, or unlawful retaliation, as in hiring, recruitment, referral for a fee, or discharge.

Citizenship discrimination covers employers with four or more employees. If you are discriminated against based on nationality (place of birth, appearance, accent, or language), you should send a complaint to:

U.S. Department of Justice
Civil Rights Division
Office of Special Counsel for
Immigration Related Unfair Employment Practices
950 Pennsylvania Avenue, NW
Washington, DC 20530
(202) 616-5594
TTY: (800) 255-8155
Employer hot line: (800) 255-8155
Employee hot line: (800) 255-7688
Fax: (202) 616-5509
www.usdoj.gov/crt/osc

The Office of Special Counsel handles cases of discrimination based on citizenship by employers with four or more employees, and national origin discrimination committed by employers with four to 14 employees. Citizenship discrimination complaints may also be sent to a district office of the **Equal Employment Opportunity Commission** listed on page 66. Lack of citizenship discrimination is not always a basis for a complaint of illegal discrimination (see page 20), since the hiring of illegal aliens is prohibited.

Recent changes in welfare and immigration laws have shifted the administration of need-based social programs and Medicaid to the states. These changes now allow states to withhold assistance from persons who are not citizens, subject to certain exemptions for refugees or asylees who have resided in the U.S. for 5 years or less; aliens serving or who have served in the military (and their spouses and dependent children); and permanent legal residents who have worked lawfully in the U.S. for at least 10 years. In addition, the new laws make permanent legal residents ineligible to receive food stamps or SSI assistance, unless they have lawfully worked in the U.S. for at least 10 years.

To find out what benefits you may be eligible to receive, contact your state's Department of Human Services or the proper office of the U.S. Department of Health and Human Services listed on page 56.

Regardless of citizenship status, if you believe you or your child has been discriminated against by a public elementary or secondary school, you should contact the U.S. Department of Education listed on page 13.

Native Americans

Through the Indian Civil Rights Act of 1968 (ICRA), Congress statutorily imposed on tribal governments provisions similar to those found in the Bill of Rights. Commonly known as the Indian Bill of Rights, the ICRA provides protections similar, but not identical, to those provided by the U.S. Constitution.

Tribal forums are available to enforce rights created by the ICRA. Federal courts do not oversee tribal compliance with the ICRA, except in cases of habeas corpus.

The American Indian Religious Freedom Act declares that a lack of clear and adequate legal protection for the religious use of peyote by Indians might serve to stigmatize Indian tribes and cultures and increase the risk that they would be exposed to discriminatory treatment. On that basis, the act preserves Indians' rights to the sacramental use of peyote.

Likewise, a 1994 presidential memorandum recognizes the sacred place of eagle feathers in Native American culture and religious practices and provides easier access to scarce eagle carcasses and parts.

Civil rights laws passed by Congress protect all citizens, including Native Americans and non-Native Americans. Therefore, any Native American can bring a discrimination complaint if he or she suffers discrimination by the federal, state, or local governments, or individuals on account of race, color, creed, religion, sex, or national origin with respect to housing, employment, commercial transactions, or access to public accommodations.

If you think you have been discriminated against because you are a Native American, you should file a complaint with the appropriate agency listed in chapter 3 of this booklet. In addition, you should write to:

U.S. Department of Justice
Assistant Attorney General for Civil Rights
950 Pennsylvania Avenue, NW
Washington, DC 20530
(202) 514-2151
Fax: (202) 514-0293
TTY: (202) 514-0216
www.usdoj.gov/crt

For further information on Department of Justice and federal government activities affecting Native Americans contact:

U.S. Department of Justice
Office of Tribal Justice
950 Pennsylvania Avenue, NW, Room 5634
Washington, DC 20530
(202) 514-8812
Fax: (202) 514-9078
www.usdoj.gov/otj

Institutionalized Persons

The Department of Justice protects your rights if you are an individual confined in certain institutions owned or operated by or on behalf of a state or local government. These institutions include facilities for the mentally ill and developmentally disabled, nursing homes for the elderly, prisons and jails, and detention halls for juveniles.

If you have a complaint, send it to:

U.S. Department of Justice
Civil Rights Division
Special Litigation Section
950 Pennsylvania Avenue, NW
Washington, DC 20530
(202) 514-6255
(877) 218-5228
Fax: (202) 514-6273

If you are an individual confined to an institution owned or operated by the federal government and have a complaint concerning staff misconduct, contact:

Federal Bureau of Prisons
Office of Internal Affairs
320 First Street, NW, Room 600
Washington, DC 20534
(202) 307-3286

Military Personnel

If you are in the **U.S. Navy** and have a discrimination complaint about an aspect of military life, it should be handled through the chain of command.

If you are in the **U.S. Army** or **Marine Corps**, discrimination complaints are handled through the chain of command and inspector general channels.

If you are in the **U.S. Air Force**, a discrimination complaint should first be taken up with your supervisor or commander. If it is not resolved to your satisfaction, you should contact the equal opportunity and treatment officer or the noncommissioned officer at your wing or base social actions office.

If you are in **any branch of the armed services** and are discriminated against in **off-base housing**, contact your post or base housing referral office. If the discriminatory act took place in the United States, you should also file a compliant with the Department of Housing and Urban Development (see page 28).

5. More Help

Discrimination Law Guides

A *Compilation of Civil Rights Laws* may be obtained free from:

U.S. Commission on Civil Rights
Publications Office
624 Ninth Street, NW, Room 600
Washington, DC 20425
(202) 376-8110
(202) 376-8128
TTY: (202) 376-8116
E-mail: publications@usccr.gov

Civil Rights Protection in the United States: Brief Summaries of Constitutional Amendments, Federal Laws and Executive Orders, prepared by the Congressional Research Service of the Library of Congress, may be obtained by contacting your congressional representative.

To obtain a comprehensive guide to the legal rights of prisoners, request *The Rights of Prisoners*, an American Civil Liberties Union handbook, by writing to:

Southern Illinois University Press
P.O. Box 3697
Carbondale, IL 62902-3697

Legal Action

It may be necessary to bring a lawsuit to enforce your rights. However, if an administrative procedure has been set up to deal with a particular problem, such as employment discrimination, courts may require you to exhaust that process before a suit can be filed.

For legal assistance, you may contact your local legal aid society.

6. Agency Regional, District, or Local Offices

BUREAU OF PRISONS REGIONAL OFFICES
Address Complaints to: Regional Director

MID-ATLANTIC REGION
Area Covered: Delaware, District of Columbia, Indiana, Kentucky, Maryland, Michigan, North Carolina, Ohio, South Carolina, Virginia, and West Virginia
302 Sentinel Drive, Suite 200
Annapolis Junction, MD 20701
(301) 317-3100
Fax: (301) 312-3115

NORTH CENTRAL REGION
Area Covered: Colorado, Illinois, Kansas, Minnesota, Missouri, Nebraska, North Dakota, South Dakota, and Wisconsin
Gateway Complex, Inc.
400 State Avenues, Suite 800
Kansas City, KS 66101
(913) 621-3939
Fax: (913) 551-1125

NORTHEAST REGION
Area Covered: Connecticut, Maine, Massachusetts, New Hampshire, New Jersey, New York, Pennsylvania, Rhode Island, and Vermont
U.S. Customs House
Second and Chestnut Streets, 7th Floor
Philadelphia, PA 19106
(215) 521-7301
Fax: (215) 521-7476

SOUTH CENTRAL REGION
Area Covered: Arkansas, Louisiana, New Mexico, Oklahoma, and Texas
4211 Cedar Springs Road, Suite 300
Dallas, TX 75219
(214) 224-3389
Fax: (214) 224-3420

SOUTHEAST REGION
Area Covered: Alabama, Florida, Georgia, Mississippi, Puerto Rico, South Carolina, and Virgin Islands
3800 Camp Creek Parkway, SW, Building 2000
Atlanta, GA 30331
(678) 686-1200
Fax: (678) 686-1229

WESTERN REGION
Area Covered: Alaska, Arizona, California, Hawaii, Idaho, Montana, Nevada, Oregon, Utah, Washington, and Wyoming
7950 Dublin Boulevard, 3rd Floor
Dublin, CA 94568
(925) 803-4700
Fax: (925) 803-4802

COMPTROLLER OF THE CURRENCY DISTRICT OFFICES
Address Complaints to: Compliance Manager

CENTRAL DISTRICT
Area Covered: Illinois, Indiana, northeast and southeast Iowa, central Kentucky, Michigan, Minnesota, eastern Missouri, Ohio, and Wisconsin
One Financial Plaza
440 South LaSalle Street, Suite 2700
Chicago, IL 60605
(312) 360-8800
TTY: (312) 360-8827

NORTHEASTERN DISTRICT
Area Covered: Connecticut, Delaware, District of Columbia, northeast Kentucky, Maine, Maryland, Massachusetts, New Hampshire, New Jersey, New York, North Carolina, Pennsylvania, Puerto Rico, Rhode Island, South Carolina, Vermont, Virgin Islands, Virginia, and West Virginia
340 Madison Avenue, 5th Floor
New York, NY 10017
(212) 790-4000
TDD: (212) 790-4084

SOUTHERN DISTRICT
Area Covered: Alabama, Arkansas, Florida, Georgia, southern Kentucky, Louisiana, Mississippi, Oklahoma, Tennessee, Texas, and West Virginia (southern)
500 N. Akard Street, Suite 1600
Dallas, TX 75201
(214) 720-0656

TDD: (214) 720-7086

WESTERN DISTRICT
Area Covered: Alaska, Arizona, California, Colorado, Guam, Hawaii, Idaho, central and western Iowa, Kansas, western Missouri, Montana, Nebraska, Nevada, New Mexico, Oregon, South Dakota, Utah, Washington, and Wyoming
1225 17th Street, Suite 300
Denver, CO 80202
(720) 475-7600
TDD: (720) 475-7697

DEPARTMENT OF EDUCATION—OCR ENFORCEMENT OFFICES
Address Complaints to: Office for Civil Rights

ENFORCEMENT DIVISION A
Area Covered: Connecticut, Maine, Massachusetts, New Hampshire, Rhode Island, and Vermont
33 Arch Street, Suite 900
Boston, MA 02110
(617) 289-0111
TTY: (877) 521-2172
Fax: (617) 289-0150

Area Covered: New Jersey, New York, Puerto Rico, and Virgin Islands
32 Old Slip, 26th Floor
New York, NY 10005
(646) 428-3900
TTY: (877) 521-2172
Fax: (646) 428-3843

Area Covered: Delaware, Maryland, Pennsylvania, West Virginia, and Kentucky
Wanawater Building
100 Pennsylvania Square East, Suite 515
Philadelphia, PA 19107
(215) 656-8541
TTY: (877) 521-2172
Fax: (215) 656-8605

ENFORCEMENT DIVISION B
Area Covered: Alabama, Florida, Georgia, and Tennessee
61 Forsyth Street, SW, Suite 19T70
Atlanta, GA 30303
(404) 562-6350
TTY: (877) 521-2172

Fax: (404) 562-6455

Area Covered: Arkansas, Louisiana, Mississippi, New Mexico, Oklahoma, and Texas
1999 Bryan Street, Suite 1620
Dallas, TX 75201
(214) 661-9600
TTY: (877) 521-2172
Fax: (214) 661-9587

ENFORCEMENT DIVISION C
Area Covered: Illinois, Indiana, Iowa, Minnesota, North Dakota, and Wisconsin
Citi Group Center
500 Madison Street, Suite 1475
Chicago, IL 60661
(312) 730-1560
TTY: (877) 521-2172
Fax: (312) 730-1576

Area Covered: Michigan and Ohio (elementary and secondary schools only)
Bank One Center
600 Superior Avenue East, Suite 750
Cleveland, OH 44114-2611
(216) 522-4970
TTY: (877) 521-2172
Fax: (216) 522-2573

Area Covered: District of Columbia, South Carolina, North Carolina, and Virginia
1100 Pennsylvania Avenue, NW, Room 316
Washington, DC 20044
(202) 786-0500
TTY: (877) 521-2172
Fax: (202) 208-7797

Area Covered: Iowa, Kansas, Missouri, Nebraska, and South Dakota
8930 Ward Parkway, Suite 2037
Kansas City, MO 64114
(816) 268-0550
TTY: (877) 521-2172
Fax: (816) 823-1404

54

ENFORCEMENT DIVISION D
Area Covered: Arizona, Colorado, New Mexico, Utah, and Wyoming
Cesar E. Chavez Memorial Building
1244 Speer Boulevard, Suite 310
Denver, CO 80204-3582
(303) 844-5695
TTY: (877) 521-2172
Fax: (303) 844-4303

Area Covered: California
50 Beale Street, Suite 7200
San Francisco, CA 94105
(415) 486-5555
TTY: (877) 521-2172
Fax: (415) 486-5570

Area Covered: Alaska, Hawaii, Idaho, Montana, Nevada, Oregon, Washington, American Samoa, and Guam
Jackson Federal Building
915 Second Avenue, Room 3310
Seattle, WA 98174-1099
(206) 220-7900
TTY: (877) 521-2172
Fax: (206) 220-7887

DEPARTMENT OF HEALTH AND HUMAN SERVICES
REGIONAL OFFICES
Address Complaints to: Office for Civil Rights

REGION I
Area Covered: Connecticut, Maine, Massachusetts, New Hampshire, Rhode Island, and Vermont
Government Center
John F. Kennedy Federal Building, Room 1875
Boston, MA 02203
(617) 565-1340
TTY: (617) 565-1343
Fax: (617) 565-3809

REGION II
Area Covered: New Jersey, New York, Puerto Rico, and Virgin Islands
Jacob Javits Federal Building
26 Federal Plaza, Suite 3312
New York, NY 10278
(212) 264-3313
TTY: (212) 264-2355
Fax: (212) 264-3039

REGION III
Area Covered: Delaware, District of Columbia, Maryland, Pennsylvania, Virginia, and West Virginia
Public Ledger Building
150 South Independence Mall West, Suite 372
Philadelphia, PA 19106
(215) 861-4441
TTY: (215) 861-4440
Fax: (215) 861-4431

REGION IV
Area Covered: Alabama, Florida, Georgia, Kentucky, Mississippi, North Carolina, South Carolina, and Tennessee
Atlanta Federal Center
61 Forsyth Street, SW, Suite 8909
Atlanta, GA 30303
(404) 562-7886
TTY: (404) 331-2867
Fax: (404) 562-7881

REGION V
Area Covered: Illinois, Indiana, Michigan, Minnesota, Ohio, and Wisconsin
233 North Michigan Avenue, Suite 280
Chicago, IL 60601
(312) 886-2359
TTY: (312) 353-5693
Fax: (312) 886-1807

REGION VI
Area Covered: Arkansas, Louisiana, New Mexico, Oklahoma, and Texas
1301 Young Street, Suite 1169
Dallas, TX 75202
(214) 767-4056
TTY: (214) 767-8940
Fax: (214) 767-0432

REGION VII
Area Covered: Iowa, Kansas, Missouri, and Nebraska
Bolling Federal Building
601 East 12th Street, Room 248
Kansas City, MO 64106
(816) 426-6367
TTY: (816) 426-7065
Fax: (816) 426-3686

REGION VIII
Area Covered: Colorado, Montana, North Dakota, South Dakota, Utah, and Wyoming
Rogers Federal Office Building
1961 Stout Street, Room 1185
Denver, CO 80294-3538
(303) 844-2024
TTY: (303) 844-3439
Fax: (303) 844-2025

REGION IX
Area Covered: American Samoa, Arizona, California, Guam, Hawaii, and Nevada
Federal Office Building
50 United Nations Plaza, Room 322
San Francisco, CA 94102
(415) 437-8310
TTY: (415) 437-8311
Fax: (415) 437-8329

REGION X
Area Covered: Alaska, Idaho, Oregon, and Washington
Blanchard Plaza Building
2201 Sixth Avenue
Seattle, WA 98121
(206) 615-2290
TTY: (206) 615-2296
Fax: (206) 615-2297

DEPARTMENT OF HOUSING AND URBAN DEVELOPMENT REGIONAL OFFICES FOR FAIR HOUSING AND EQUAL OPPORTUNITY
Address Complaints to: Director

BOSTON REGIONAL OFFICE
Covers: Connecticut, Maine, Massachusetts, New Hampshire, Rhode Island, and Vermont
Fair Housing and Equal Opportunity
U.S. Department of Housing and Urban Development
Thomas P. O'Neill, Jr. Federal Building
10 Causeway Street, Room 321
Boston, MA 02222
(617) 994-8300
(800) 827-5005
TTY: (617) 565-5453

NEW YORK REGIONAL OFFICE
Covers: New York and New Jersey
Fair Housing and Equal Opportunity
U.S. Department of Housing and Urban Development
Jacob K. Javits Federal Building
26 Federal Plaza
New York, NY 10278-0068
(212) 542-7519
(800) 496-4294
TTY: (212) 264-0927

PHILADELPHIA REGIONAL OFFICE
Covers: Delaware, District of Columbia, Maryland, Pennsylvania, Virginia, and West Virginia
Fair Housing and Equal Opportunity
U.S. Department of Housing and Urban Development
The Wanamaker Building
100 Penn Square East
Philadelphia, PA 19107
(215) 861-7647
(888) 799-2085
TTY: (215) 656-3450

ATLANTA REGIONAL OFFICE
Covers: Alabama, Caribbean, Florida, Georgia, Kentucky, Mississippi, North Carolina, South Carolina, Tennessee, and Puerto Rico
Fair Housing and Equal Opportunity
U.S. Department of Housing and Urban Development
Five Points Plaza
40 Marietta Street, 16th Floor
Atlanta, GA 30303
(404) 331-5140
(800) 440-8091
TTY: (404) 730-2654

CHICAGO REGIONAL OFFICE
Covers: Illinois, Indiana, Michigan, Minnesota, Ohio, and Wisconsin
Fair Housing and Equal Opportunity
U.S. Department of Housing and Urban Development
Ralph H. Metcalfe Federal Building
77 West Jackson Boulevard
Chicago, IL 60604
 (312) 353-7776 ext. 2453
(800) 765-9372
TTY: (312) 353-7143

FORT WORTH REGIONAL OFFICE
Covers: Arkansas, Louisiana, New Mexico, Oklahoma, and Texas
Fair Housing and Equal Opportunity
U.S. Department of Housing and Urban Development
801 Cherry Street, 27th Floor
Fort Worth, TX 76113-2905
(817) 978-5900
(800) 669-9777
TTY: (817) 978-5595

KANSAS CITY REGIONAL OFFICE
Covers: Iowa, Kansas, Missouri, and Nebraska
Fair Housing Enforcement Center
U.S. Department of Housing and Urban Development
Gateway Tower II
400 State Avenue, Room 200
Kansas City, KS 66101
(913) 551-6958
(800) 743-5323
TTY: (913) 551-6972

DENVER REGIONAL OFFICE
Covers: Colorado, Montana, North Dakota, South Dakota, Utah, and Wyoming
Fair Housing and Equal Opportunity
U.S. Department of Housing and Urban Development
1670 Broadway
Denver, CO 80202
(303) 672-5437
(800) 877-7353
TTY: (303) 672-5248

SAN FRANCISCO REGIONAL OFFICE
Covers: Arizona, California, Hawaii, and Nevada
Fair Housing and Equal Opportunity
U.S. Department of Housing and Urban Development
600 Harrison Street, 3rd Floor
San Francisco, CA 94107
(415) 489-6524
(800) 347-3739
TTY: (415) 436-6594

SEATTLE REGIONAL OFFICE
Covers: Alaska, Idaho, Oregon, Washington
Area Office: Spokane, and Washington
Fair Housing and Equal Opportunity
U.S. Department of Housing and Urban Development
909 First Avenue, Suite 205
Seattle, WA 98104
(206) 220-5170
(800) 877-0246
TTY: (206) 220-5185

DEPARTMENT OF LABOR REGIONAL OFFICES

**Office of Federal Contract Compliance Programs (OFCCP),
Employment Standards Administration**
**Address Complaints concerning federal contractors to: Regional
Director, OFCCP/ESA**

NORTHEAST REGION
**Area Covered: Connecticut, Maine, Massachusetts, New Hampshire,
Rhode Island, Vermont, New Jersey, New York, Puerto Rico, and Virgin
Islands**
201 Varick Street, Room 750
New York, NY 10014
(646) 264-3170
Fax: (646) 264-3009

MID-ATLANTIC REGION
**Area Covered: Delaware, District of Columbia, Maryland, Pennsylvania,
Virginia, and West Virginia**
Curtis Center
170 South Independence Mall West, Suite 750W
Philadelphia, PA 19106
(215) 861-5765
Fax: (215) 861-5769

SOUTHEAST REGION
**Area Covered: Alabama, Florida, Georgia, Kentucky, Mississippi, North
Carolina, South Carolina, and Tennessee**
Atlanta Federal Center
61 Forsyth Street, SW, Room 7B75
Atlanta, GA 30303
(404) 893-4545
Fax: (404) 893-4546

MIDWEST REGION
**Area Covered: Illinois, Indiana, Iowa, Kansas, Michigan, Minnesota,
Missouri, Nebraska, Ohio, and Wisconsin**
Kluczynski Federal Building
230 South Dearborn Street, Room 570
Chicago, IL 60604
(312) 596-7010
Fax: (312) 596-7037

SOUTHWEST/ROCKY MOUNTAIN REGION
Area Covered: Arkansas, Colorado, Louisiana, Montana, New Mexico, North Dakota, Oklahoma, South Dakota, Texas, Utah, and Wyoming
Federal Building
525 South Griffin Street, Room 840
Dallas, TX 75202-5007
(972) 850-2550
Fax: (972) 850-2552

PACIFIC REGION
Area Covered: Alaska, Arizona, California, Guam, Hawaii, Idaho, Nevada, Oregon, and Washington
90 7th Street, Suite 18-30
San Francisco, CA 94102
(415) 625-7800
Fax: (415) 625-7799

Address Complaints concerning family and medical leave to: Regional Administrator, Wage and Hour Division/ESA

BOSTON
Area Covered: Connecticut, Maine, Massachusetts, New Hampshire, Rhode Island, and Vermont
J.F.K. Federal Building, Room E-350
Boston, MA 02203
(617) 565-3630
Fax: (617) 562-2999

NEW YORK REGION
Area Covered: New Jersey, New York, Puerto Rico, and Virgin Islands
26 Federal Plaza, Room 3700
New York, NY 10278
(212) 264-8185
Fax: (212) 264-9548

PHILADELPHIA REGION
Area Covered: Delaware, District of Columbia, Maryland, Pennsylvania, Virginia, and West Virginia
170 South Independence Mall West, Room 850W
Philadelphia, PA 19106
(215) 861-5800
Fax: (215) 861-5840

ATLANTA REGION
Area Covered: Alabama, Florida, Georgia, Kentucky, Mississippi, North Carolina, South Carolina, and Tennessee
61 Forsyth Street, SW, Room 6M12
Atlanta, GA 30303
(404) 562-2092
Fax: (404) 562-2149

CHICAGO REGION
Area Covered: Illinois, Indiana, Michigan, Minnesota, Ohio, and Wisconsin
230 Dearborn Street, Room 638
Chicago, IL 60604-1591
(312) 353-0301
Fax: (312) 353-4474

DALLAS REGION
Area Covered: Arkansas, Colorado, Louisiana, Montana, New Mexico, North Dakota, Oklahoma, South Dakota, Texas, Utah, and Wyoming
525 Griffin Street, Room 317
Dallas, TX 75202
(219) 767-8263
Fax: (219) 767-5113

KANSAS CITY REGION
Area Covered: Iowa, Kansas, Missouri, and Nebraska
1222 Spruce Street, Room 9102B
St. Louis, MO 63103-2830
(314) 539-2706
Fax: (314) 539-2223

SAN FRANCISCO REGION
Area Covered: Alaska, Arizona, California, Hawaii, Idaho, Nevada, Oregon, and Washington
455 Market Street, Suite 800
San Francisco, CA 94105
(415) 744-5590
Fax: (415) 744-5088

Address Complaints concerning state employment services, unemployment benefits office, and training programs to: Regional Administrator, Employment and Training Administration

REGION I
Area Covered: Connecticut, Maine, Massachusetts, New Hampshire, Rhode Island, and Vermont
J.F.K. Federal Building, Room E-350
Boston, MA 02203
(617) 565-3630
Fax: (617) 565-2999

REGION II
Area Covered: New Jersey, New York, Puerto Rico, and Virgin Islands
201 Varick Street, Room 755
New York, NY 10014
(212) 337-2139
Fax: (212) 337-2144

REGION III
Area Covered: Delaware, District of Columbia, Maryland, Pennsylvania, Virginia, and West Virginia
The Curtis Center
170 South Independence Mall West, Suite 825E
Philadelphia, PA 19106-3315
(215) 861-5200
Fax: (215) 861-5260

REGION IV
Area Covered: Alabama, Florida, Georgia, Kentucky, Mississippi, North Carolina, South Carolina, and Tennessee
61 Forsyth Street, Room 7B75
Atlanta, GA 30303
(404) 562-2092
Fax: (404) 562-2149

REGION V
Area Covered: Illinois, Indiana, Michigan, Minnesota, Ohio, and Wisconsin
Kluczynski Building
230 South Dearborn Street, Room 628
Chicago, IL 60604
(312) 353-0313
Fax: (312) 353-4474

REGION VI
Area Covered: Arkansas, Louisiana, New Mexico, Oklahoma, and Texas
235 Griffin Street, Room 317
Dallas, TX 75202
(214) 767-8263
Fax: (214) 767-5113

REGION VII
Area Covered: Iowa, Kansas, Missouri, and Nebraska
City Center Square
1100 Main Street, Suite 1050
Kansas City, MO 64105
(816) 502-9000
Fax: (816) 502-9001

REGION VIII
**Area Covered: Colorado, Montana, North Dakota, South Dakota, Utah,
and Wyoming**
1999 Broadway, Room 1780
Denver, CO 80202
(303) 844-1651

REGION IX
Area Covered: Arizona, California, Hawaii, and Nevada
71 Stevenson Street, Suite 830
San Francisco, CA 94119
(415) 975-4610
Fax: (415) 975-4612

REGION X
Area Covered: Alaska, Idaho, Oregon, and Washington
1111 Third Avenue, Suite 815
Seattle, WA 98101-3212
(206) 553-7700
Fax: (206) 553-0098

EQUAL EMPLOYMENT OPPORTUNITY COMMISSION
DISTRICT OFFICES, FIELD OFFICES, AND AREA OFFICES
Address Complaints to: District, Field, or Area Director, EEOC

ALBUQUERQUE AREA OFFICE
Area Covered: New Mexico
505 Marquette Street, NW, Suite 900
Albuquerque, NM 87102
(505) 248-5201
(800) 669-4000
TTY: (800) 669-6820
Fax: (505) 248-5239

ATLANTA DISTRICT OFFICE
Area Covered: Georgia
100 Alabama Street, SW, Suite 4R30
Atlanta, GA 30303
(404) 562-6800
(800) 669-4000
TTY: (800) 669-6820
Fax: (404) 562-6909

BALTIMORE FIELD OFFICE
Area Covered: Maryland and Virginia
City Crescent Building
10 South Howard Street, 3rd Floor
Baltimore, MD 21201
(410) 962-3932
(800) 669-4000
TTY: (800) 669-6820
Fax: (410) 962-4270

BIRMINGHAM DISTRICT OFFICE
Area Covered: Alabama and Mississippi
1130 22nd Street, Suite 2000
Birmingham, AL 32205-2397
(205) 731-0082
(800) 669-4000
TTY: (800) 669-6820
Fax: (205) 731-2105

CHARLOTTE DISTRICT OFFICE
Area Covered: North Carolina, South Carolina, and Virginia (Southern)
129 West Trade Street, Suite 400
Charlotte, NC 28202
(704) 344-6682
(800) 669-4000
TTY: (800) 669-6820
Fax: (704) 344-6734

CHICAGO DISTRICT OFFICE
Area Covered: Illinois (Northern)
500 West Madison Street, Suite 2800
Chicago, IL 60661
(312) 353-2713
(800) 669-4000
TTY: (800) 669-6820
Fax: (312) 886-1168

CLEVELAND FIELD OFFICE
Area Covered: Ohio
1240 E. 9TH Street, Suite 3001
Cleveland, OH 44199
(216) 522-2001
(800) 669-4000
TTY: (800) 669-6820
Fax: (216) 522-7395

DALLAS DISTRICT OFFICE
Area Covered: Oklahoma and Texas (Northern)
207 South Houston, 3rd Floor
Dallas, TX 75202-4726
(214) 655-3355
(800) 669-4000
TTY: (800) 669-6820
Fax: (214) 655-3433

DENVER FIELD OFFICE
Area Covered: Colorado and Wyoming
303 East 17th Avenue, Suite 510
Denver, CO 80203-9634
(303) 866-1300
(800) 669-4000
TTY: (800) 669-6820
Fax: (303) 566-1085

DETROIT FIELD OFFICE
Area Covered: Michigan
Patrick V. McNamara Federal Building
477 Michigan Avenue, Room 865
Detroit, MI 48226
(313) 226-4600
(800) 669-4000
TTY: (800) 669-6820
Fax: (313) 226-4610

HOUSTON DISTRICT OFFICE
Area Covered: Texas (Central)
Mickey Leland Federal Building
1919 Smith Street, Suite 600
Houston, TX 77002
(713) 209-3320
(800) 669-4000
TTY: (800) 669-6820
Fax: (713) 209-3381

INDIANAPOLIS DISTRICT OFFICE
Area Covered: Indiana and Kentucky
101 West Ohio Street, Suite 1900
Indianapolis, IN 46204
(317) 226-7212
(800) 669-4000
TTY: (800) 669-6820
Fax: (317) 226-7953

LOS ANGELES DISTRICT OFFICE
Area Covered: California (Southern) and Nevada
Roybal Federal Building
255 East Temple, 4th Floor
Los Angeles, CA 90012
(213) 894-1000
(800) 669-4000
TTY: (800) 669-6820
Fax: (213) 894-1118

MEMPHIS DISTRICT OFFICE
Area Covered: Arkansas and Tennessee
1407 Union Avenue, Suite 621
Memphis, TN 38104
(901) 544-0115
(800) 669-4000
TTY: (800) 669-6820
Fax: (901) 544-0111

MIAMI DISTRICT OFFICE
Area Covered: Florida and Panama Canal Zone
One Biscayne Tower
Two South Biscayne Boulevard, Suite 2700
Miami, FL 33131
(305) 536-4491
(800) 669-4000
TTY: (800) 669-6820
Fax: (305) 808-1855

MILWAUKEE AREA OFFICE
Area Covered: Iowa, Minnesota and Wisconsin
Henry S. Reuss Federal Plaza
310 West Wisconsin Avenue, Suite 800
Milwaukee, WI 53203
(414) 297-1111
(800) 669-4000
TTY: (800) 669-6820
Fax: (414) 297-4133

NEW ORLEANS FIELD OFFICE
Area Covered: Louisiana
1555 Poydras Street, Suite 1900
New Orleans, LA 70113
(800) 669-4000
TTY: (800) 669-6820
Fax: (504) 595-2887

NEW YORK DISTRICT FIELD OFFICE
Area Covered: Connecticut, Maine, Massachusetts, New Hampshire, New York, Puerto Rico, Rhode Island, Vermont, and Virgin Islands
33 Whitehall Street, 5th Floor
New York, NY 10004-2112
(212) 336-3620
(800) 669-4000TTY: (800) 669-6820

PHILADELPHIA DISTRICT OFFICE
Area Covered: Delaware, New Jersey, Pennsylvania, and West Virginia
21 South Fifth Street, Suite 400
Philadelphia, PA 19106
(215) 440-2600
(800) 669-4000
TTY: (800) 669-6820
Fax: (215) 440-2606

PHOENIX DISTRICT OFFICE
Area Covered: Arizona and Utah
3300 North Central Avenue, Suite 690
Phoenix, AZ 85012
(602) 640-5000
(800) 669-4000
TTY: (800) 669-6820
Fax: (602) 640-5071

ST. LOUIS DISTRICT OFFICE
Area Covered: Kansas, Missouri, and Illinois (Alexander, Bond, Calhoun, Clinton, Greene, Jackson, Jersey, Macoupin, Madison, Monroe, Perry, Pulaski, Randolph, St. Clair, Union, and Washington Counties)
1222 Spruce, Suite 8100
St. Louis, MO 63103
(314) 539-7800
(800) 669-4000
TTY: (800) 669-6820
Fax: (314) 539-7894

SAN ANTONIO FIELD OFFICE
Area Covered: Texas (Southern)
5410 Fredericksburg Road, Suite 200
San Antonio, TX 78229
(210) 281-7600
(800) 669-4000
TTY: (800) 669-6820
Fax: (210) 281-7690

SAN FRANCISCO DISTRICT OFFICE
Area Covered: American Samoa, California (Northern), Commonwealth of the Northern Mariana Islands, Guam, Hawaii, and Wake Island
350 The Embarcadero, Suite 500
San Francisco, CA 94105
(800) 669-4000
TTY: (800) 669-6820
Fax: (415) 625-5609

SEATTLE FIELD OFFICE
Area Covered: Alaska, Idaho, Oregon, and Washington
909 First Avenue, Suite 400
Seattle, WA 98104-1061
(206) 220-6883
(800) 669-4000
TTY: (800) 669-6820
Fax: (206) 220-6911

WASHINGTON (DC) FIELD OFFICE
Area Covered: District of Columbia, and Virginia (Northern)
1400 L Street, NW, Suite 200
Washington, DC 20005
(800) 669-4000
TTY: (800) 669-6820
Fax: (202) 419-0740

FEDERAL DEPOSIT INSURANCE CORPORATION
REGIONAL OFFICES
Address Complaints to: Regional Director

ATLANTA REGION
Area Covered: Alabama, Florida, Georgia, North Carolina, South Carolina, Virginia, and West Virginia
10 Tenth Street, NE, Suite 800
Atlanta, GA 30309
(678) 916-2200
(800) 765-3342

BOSTON REGION
Area Covered: Connecticut, Maine, Massachusetts, New Hampshire, Rhode Island, and Vermont
15 Braintree Hill Office Park, Suite 100
Braintree, MA 02184
(781) 794-5500

CHICAGO REGION
Area Covered: Illinois, Indiana, Kentucky, Michigan, Ohio, and Wisconsin
500 West Monroe Street, Room 3300
Chicago, IL 60661
(312) 382-6000
Fax: (312) 382-6901

DALLAS REGION
Area Covered: Colorado, New Mexico, Oklahoma, and Texas
1910 Pacific Avenue, 20th Floor
Dallas, TX 75201
(214) 754-0098
(800) 568-9161

KANSAS CITY REGION
Area Covered: Iowa, Kansas, Minnesota, Missouri, Nebraska, North Dakota, and South Dakota
2345 Grand Boulevard, Suite 1200
Kansas City, MO 64108
(816) 234-8000
(800) 209-7459

MEMPHIS REGION
Area Covered: Arkansas, Louisiana, Mississippi, and Tennessee
5100 Poplar Avenue, Suite 1900
Memphis, TN 38137
(901) 685-1603
(800) 210-6354

NEW YORK REGION
Area Covered: Delaware, District of Columbia, Maryland, New Jersey, New York, Pennsylvania, Puerto Rico, and Virgin Islands
20 Exchange Place, 4th Floor
New York, NY 10005
(917) 320-2500
(800) 334-9593

SAN FRANCISCO REGION
Area Covered: Alaska, Arizona, California, Guam, Hawaii, Idaho, Montana, Nevada, Oregon, Utah, Washington, and Wyoming
25 Jessie Street at Ecker Square, Suite 2300
San Francisco, CA 94105
(415) 846-0160
(800) 756-3558

FEDERAL RESERVE BANKS BY DISTRICT
Address Complaints to: Vice President for Community Affairs

FIRST DISTRICT—BOSTON
Area Covered: Connecticut, Maine, Massachusetts, New Hampshire, and Rhode Island, Vermont
Federal Reserve Bank of Boston
P.O. Box 55882
Boston, MA 02205
(617) 973-3000

SECOND DISTRICT—NEW YORK
Area Covered: Connecticut (Fairfield County), New Jersey (Northern), and New York
Federal Reserve Bank of New York
33 Liberty Street
New York, NY 10045
(212) 720-5000

THIRD DISTRICT—PHILADELPHIA
Area Covered: Delaware, New Jersey (Southern), and Pennsylvania (Eastern)
Federal Reserve Bank of Philadelphia
10 Independence Mall
Philadelphia, PA 19106
(215) 574-6000

FOURTH DISTRICT—CLEVELAND
Area Covered: Kentucky (Eastern), Ohio, Pennsylvania (Western), and West Virginia (Northern Panhandle)
Federal Reserve Bank of Cleveland
1455 East Sixth Street
Cleveland, OH 44114
(216) 579-2000

FIFTH DISTRICT—RICHMOND
Area Covered: District of Columbia, Maryland, North Carolina, South Carolina, Virginia, and West Virginia (except Northern Panhandle)
Federal Reserve Bank of Richmond
701 East Byrd Street
Richmond, VA 23219
(804) 697-8000

SIXTH DISTRICT—ATLANTA
Area Covered: Alabama, Florida, Georgia, Louisiana (Southern), Mississippi (Southern), and Tennessee (Eastern Two-Thirds)
1000 Peachtree Street, NE
Atlanta, GA 30309-4470
(404) 498-8500

SEVENTH DISTRICT—CHICAGO
Area Covered: Illinois (Northern) Indiana (Northern), Iowa, Michigan, and Wisconsin (Southern)
Federal Reserve Bank of Chicago
230 South LaSalle Street
Chicago, IL 60604
(312) 322-5322

EIGHTH DISTRICT—ST. LOUIS
Area Covered: Arkansas, Illinois (Southern), Indiana (Southern), Kentucky (Western), Mississippi (Northern), Missouri (Eastern), and Tennessee (Western One-Third)
Federal Reserve Bank of St. Louis
411 Locust Street
St. Louis, MO 63102
(314) 444-8444

NINTH DISTRICT—MINNEAPOLIS
Area Covered: Michigan (Upper Peninsula), Minnesota, Montana, North Dakota, South Dakota, and Wisconsin (Northern)
Federal Reserve Bank of Minneapolis
90 Hennepin Avenue
Minneapolis, MN 55401 (612) 204-5000

TENTH DISTRICT—KANSAS CITY
Area Covered: Colorado, Kansas, Missouri (Western), Nebraska, New Mexico (Northern), Oklahoma, and Wyoming
Federal Reserve Bank of Kansas City
925 Grand Boulevard
Kansas City, MO 64198
(816) 881-2000

ELEVENTH DISTRICT—DALLAS
Area Covered: Louisiana (Northern), New Mexico (Southern), and Texas
Federal Reserve Bank of Dallas
2200 North Pearl Street
Dallas, TX 75201
(214) 922-6000

TWELFTH DISTRICT—SAN FRANCISCO
Area Covered: Alaska, Arizona, California, Hawaii, Idaho, Nevada,
Oregon, Utah, and Washington
Federal Reserve Bank of San Francisco
101 Market Street
San Francisco, CA 94105
Mail Address: P.O. Box 7702
San Francisco, CA 94120
(415) 974-2000

MERIT SYSTEMS PROTECTION BOARD
REGIONAL AND FIELD OFFICES
Address Complaints to: Chief Administrative Judge

ATLANTA REGIONAL OFFICE
Area Covered: Alabama, Florida, Georgia, Mississippi, South Carolina,
and Tennessee
Peachtree Summit Federal Building
401 West Peachtree Street, NW, 10th Floor
Atlanta, GA 30308-3519
(404) 730-2755
Fax: (404) 730-2767

CHICAGO REGIONAL OFFICE
Area Covered: Illinois (all locations north of Springfield), Indiana,
Michigan, Minnesota, Ohio, and Wisconsin
Kluczynski Federal Building
230 South Dearborn Street, Suite 3100
Chicago, IL 60604-1669
(312) 353-2923
Fax: (312) 886-4231

DALLAS REGIONAL OFFICE
Area Covered: Arkansas, Louisiana, Oklahoma, and Texas
Earl Cabell Federal Building
1100 Commerce Street, Room 620
Dallas, TX 75242-9979
(214) 767-0555
Fax: (214) 767-0102

DENVER FIELD OFFICE
Area Covered: Arizona, Colorado, Kansas (except Kansas City, KS), Montana, Nebraska, New Mexico, North Dakota, South Dakota, Utah, and Wyoming
165 South Union Boulevard, Suite 318
Lakewood, CO 80228
(303) 969-5101
Fax: (303) 969-5109

PHILADELPHIA REGIONAL OFFICE
Area Covered: Delaware; Maryland (Baltimore City and Alleghany, Anne Arundel, Baltimore, Calvert, Caroline, Carroll, Cecil, Charles, Dorchester, Frederick, Garrett, Harford, Kent, Queen Anne's, Somerset, St. Mary's, Talbot, Washington, Wicomico, and Worcester Counties); New Jersey (Atlantic, Burlington, Camden, Cape May, Cumberland, Gloucester, Hunterdon, Mercer, Middlesex, Monmouth, Morris, Ocean, Passaic, Salem, Somerset, Sussex, and Warren Counties); Pennsylvania; and West Virginia
U.S. Customs House
200 Chestnut Street, Room 501
Philadelphia, PA 19106-2987
(215) 597-9960
Fax: (215) 597-3456

BOSTON FIELD OFFICE
Area Covered: Connecticut, Maine, Massachusetts, New Hampshire, Rhode Island, and Vermont
99 Summer Street, Suite 1810
Boston, MA 02110-1200
(617) 424-5700
Fax: (617) 424-5708

NEW YORK FIELD OFFICE
Area Covered: New Jersey (Bergen, Essex, Hudson, and Union Counties), New York, Puerto Rico, and Virgin Islands
Jacob K. Javits Federal Building
26 Federal Plaza, Room 3137A
New York, NY 10278-0022
(212) 264-9372
Fax: (212) 264-1417

SAN FRANCISCO REGIONAL OFFICE
Area Covered: California and Nevada
250 Montgomery Street, Suite 400
San Francisco, CA 94104-3401
(415) 705-2935
Fax: (415) 705-2945

SEATTLE FIELD OFFICE
Area Covered: Alaska, Hawaii, Idaho, Oregon, Pacific overseas areas, and Washington
Jackson Federal Building
915 Second Avenue, Room 1840
Seattle, WA 98174-1056
(206) 220-7975
Fax: (206) 220-7982

WASHINGTON REGIONAL OFFICE
Area Covered: District of Columbia, Maryland (Montgomery and Prince Georges Counties), North Carolina, and Virginia
1800 Diagonal Road, Suite 205
Alexandria, VA 22314
(703) 756-6250
Fax: (703) 756-7112

NATIONAL CREDIT UNION ADMINISTRATION REGIONAL OFFICES
Address Complaints to: Regional Director

REGION I—ALBANY
Area Covered: Connecticut, Maine, Massachusetts, New Hampshire, New York, Rhode Island, and Vermont
9 Washington Square
Washington Avenue Extension
Albany, NY 12205
(518) 862-7400
Fax: (518) 862-7420

REGION II—CAPITAL
Area Covered: Delaware, District of Columbia, Maryland, New Jersey, Pennsylvania, Virginia, and West Virginia
1775 Duke Street, Suite 4206
Alexandria, VA 22314-3437
(703) 519-4600
Fax: (703) 519-4620

REGION III—ATLANTA
Area Covered: Alabama, Florida, Georgia, Indiana, Kentucky, Louisiana, Mississippi, North Carolina, Puerto Rico, South Carolina, Tennessee, and Virgin Islands
7000 Central Parkway, Suite 1600
Atlanta, GA 30328
(678) 443-3000
Fax: (678) 443-3020

REGION IV—AUSTIN
Area Covered: Arizona, Arkansas, Colorado, Illinois, Iowa, Kansas, Louisiana, Minnesota, Missouri, Nebraska, North Dakota, Oklahoma, South Dakota, Texas, and Wisconsin
4807 Spicewood Springs Road, Suite 5200
Austin, TX 78759
(512) 342-5600
Fax: (512) 342-5620

REGION V—TEMPE
Area Covered: Alaska, Arizona, California, Colorado, Guam, Hawaii, Idaho, Montana, Nevada, New Mexico, Oregon, Utah, Washington, and Wyoming
1230 W, Washington Street, Suite 301
Tempe, AZ 85281
(602) 302-6000
Fax: (602) 302-6024

OFFICE OF THRIFT SUPERVISION REGIONAL OFFICES
Address Complaints to: Consumer Affairs

NORTHEAST REGION
Area Covered: Connecticut, Delaware, Maine, Massachusetts, New Hampshire, New Jersey, New York, Pennsylvania, Rhode Island, Vermont, and West Virginia
Harborside Financial Center
Plaza 5, Suite 1600
Jersey City, NJ 07311
(201) 413-1000
(800) 523-2181
Fax: (201) 413-7541

SOUTHEAST REGION
Area Covered: Alabama, District of Columbia, Florida, Georgia, Kentucky, Maryland, North Carolina, Puerto Rico, South Carolina, Tennessee, Virginia, and Virgin Islands
PO Box 105217
Atlanta, GA 30348-5217
(404) 888-0771
Fax: (404) 888-8599

CENTRAL REGION
Area Covered: Illinois, Indiana, Michigan, Ohio, and Wisconsin
One South Wacker Drive, Suite 2000
Chicago, IL 60606
(312) 917-5000

MIDWEST REGION
Area Covered: Arkansas, Colorado, Iowa, Kansas, Louisiana, Minnesota, Mississippi, Missouri, Nebraska, North Dakota, New Mexico, Oklahoma, South Dakota, and Texas
225 East John Carpenter Freeway, Suite 500
Irving, TX 75062-2326
(972) 277-9500
(972) 277-9565 (Spanish)
Fax: (972) 277-9563

WEST REGION
Area Covered: Alaska, Arizona, California, Colorado, Guam, Hawaii, Idaho, Montana, Nevada, Oregon, Utah, Washington, and Wyoming
P.O. Box 7165
San Francisco, CA 94120
(650) 746-7000
(650) 746-7097 (Spanish)
Fax: (650) 746-7001

UNITED STATES ATTORNEYS' OFFICES
Address Complaints to: United States Attorney

ALABAMA—MIDDLE DISTRICT
131 Clay Street
Montgomery, AL 36104
 (334) 223-7280
Fax: (334) 223-7560

ALABAMA—NORTHERN DISTRICT
Vance Federal Building
1801 Fourth Avenue, North
Birmingham, AL 35203
(205) 244-2001
Fax: (205) 244-2171

ALABAMA—SOUTHERN DISTRICT
Riverview Plaza
63 South Royal Street, Suite 600
Mobile, AL 36602
(251) 441-5845
Fax: (251) 441-5277

ALASKA
Federal Building and U.S. Courthouse
222 West Seventh Avenue, #9, Room 253
Anchorage, AK 99513-7567
(907) 271-5071
Fax: (907) 271-3224

ARIZONA
Two Renaissance Square
40 North Central Avenue, Suite 1200
Phoenix, AZ 85004-4408
(602) 514-7500
Fax: (602) 514-7693

ARKANSAS—EASTERN DISTRICT
P.O. Box 1229
Little Rock, AR 72203
(501) 340-2600
Fax: (501) 340-2728

ARKANSAS—WESTERN DISTRICT
414 Parker Street
Fort Smith, AR 72901
 (479) 783-5125
Fax: (501) 783-2442

CALIFORNIA—CENTRAL DISTRICT
1200 U.S. Courthouse
312 North Spring Street
Los Angeles, CA 90012
(213) 894-2434
Fax: (213) 894-0141

CALIFORNIA—EASTERN DISTRICT
501 I Street, Suite 10-100
Sacramento, CA 95814
(916) 554-2700
Fax: (916) 554-2900

CALIFORNIA—NORTHERN DISTRICT
U.S. Courthouse
450 Golden Gate Avenue, Box 36055
San Francisco, CA 94102
(415) 436-7200
Fax: (415) 436-7234

CALIFORNIA—SOUTHERN DISTRICT
Federal Office Building
880 Front Street, Room 6293
San Diego, CA 92101-8893
(619) 557-5610
Fax: (619) 557-5782

COLORADO
Seventeenth Street Plaza
1225 17th Street, Suite 700
Denver, CO 80202
(303) 454-0100
Fax: (303) 454-0409

CONNECTICUT
Connecticut Financial Center
157 Church Street, 23rd Floor
New Haven, CT 06510
 (203) 821-3700
Fax: (203) 773-5376

DELAWARE
P.O. Box 2046
Wilmington, Delaware 19899-2046
(302) 573-6277
Fax: (302) 573-6220

DISTRICT OF COLUMBIA
Judiciary Center Building
555 Fourth Street, NW
Washington, DC 20530
(202) 514-7566
Fax: (202) 307-3569

81

FLORIDA—MIDDLE DISTRICT
Robert Timberlake Federal Building
400 North Tampa Street, Suite 3200
Tampa, FL 33602
(813) 274-6000
Fax: (813) 274-6246

FLORIDA—NORTHERN DISTRICT
111 North Adams Street, Suite 400
Tallahassee, FL 32301
(850) 942-8430
Fax: (850) 942-9577

FLORIDA—SOUTHERN DISTRICT
Federal Justice Building
99 Northeast Fourth Street
Miami, FL 33132
(305) 961-9000
Fax: (305) 530-7087

GEORGIA—MIDDLE DISTRICT
300 Mulberry Street, 400
Macon, GA 31201
 (478) 752-3511
Fax: (478) 621-2604

GEORGIA—NORTHERN DISTRICT
600 US Courthouse
75 Spring Street, SW, Suite 1800
Atlanta, GA 30303
(404) 581-6000
Fax: (404) 581-6181

GEORGIA—SOUTHERN DISTRICT
P.O. Box 8970
Savannah, GA 31412
(912) 652-4422
Fax: (912) 652-4388

GUAM
Sirena Plaza
108 Hernan Cortez, Suite 500
Hagatna, Guam 96910
(671) 472-7332
Fax: (671) 472-7334

HAWAII
Prince Jonah Kuhio Kalanianaole Federal Building
300 Ala Moana Boulevard, Room 6-100
Honolulu, HI 96850
 (808) 541-2850
Fax: (808) 541-2958

IDAHO
Washington Group Plaza
800 Park Boulevard, Suite 600
Boise, ID 83712
 (208) 334-1211
Fax: (208) 334-1413

ILLINOIS—CENTRAL DISTRICT
318 South Sixth Street
Springfield, IL 62701
(217) 492-4450
Fax: (217) 492-4512

ILLINOIS—NORTHERN DISTRICT
Dirksen Federal Building
219 South Dearborn Street, 5th Floor
Chicago, IL 60604
(312) 353-5300
Fax: (312) 353-2067

ILLINOIS—SOUTHERN DISTRICT
9 Executive Drive, Suite 300
Fairview Heights, IL 62208
(618) 628-3700
Fax: (618) 628-3730

INDIANA—NORTHERN DISTRICT
5400 Federal Plaza
Hammond, IN 46320
(219) 937-5500
Fax: (219) 852-2770

INDIANA—SOUTHERN DISTRICT
10 West Market Street, Suite 2100
Indianapolis, IN 46204
(317) 226-6333
Fax: (317) 226-6125

IOWA—NORTHERN DISTRICT
401 First Street, SE, Suite 400
Cedar Rapids, IA 52401
(319) 363-6333
Fax: (319) 363-1990

IOWA—SOUTHERN DISTRICT
U.S. Courthouse Annex
110 East Court Avenue, Suite 286
Des Moines, IA 50309
(515) 284-6257
Fax: (515) 284-6288

KANSAS
Epic Center
301 North Main, Suite 1200
Wichita, KS 67202-4812
(316) 269-6481
Fax: (316) 269-6484

KENTUCKY—EASTERN DISTRICT
110 West Vine Street, Room 400
Lexington, KY 40507
(859) 233-2661
Fax: (859) 233-2666

KENTUCKY—WESTERN DISTRICT
Bank of Louisville Building
510 West Broadway, 10th Floor
Louisville, KY 40202
(502) 582-5911
Fax: (502) 582-5097

LOUISIANA—EASTERN DISTRICT

500 Poydras Street, Room B210
New Orleans, LA 70130
(504) 680-3000
Fax: (504) 589-3594

LOUISIANA—MIDDLE DISTRICT
Russell B. Long Federal Building and Courthouse
777 Florida Street, Room 208
Baton Rouge, LA 70801
(225) 389-0443
Fax: (225) 389-0561

LOUISIANA—WESTERN DISTRICT
300 Fannin Street, Suite 3201
Shreveport, LA 71101-3068
(318) 676-3600
Fax: (318) 676-3641

MAINE
East Tower
100 Middle Street, 6th Floor
Portland, ME 04101
(207) 780-3257
Fax: (207) 780-3304

MARYLAND
36 South Charles Street, 4th Floor
Baltimore, MD 21201
(410) 209-4800
Fax: (410) 962-0122

MASSACHUSETTS
U.S. Courthouse
1 Courthouse Way, Suite 9200
Boston, MA 02210
(617) 748-3100
Fax: (617) 748-3953

MICHIGAN—EASTERN DISTRICT
Federal Building
211 West Fort Street, Suite 2001
Detroit, MI 48226
(313) 226-9100
Fax: (313) 226-4609

MICHIGAN—WESTERN DISTRICT
P.O. Box 208
Grand Rapids, MI 49501
(616) 456-2404
Fax: (616) 456-2408

MINNESOTA
600 U.S. Courthouse
300 South Fourth Street
Minneapolis, MN 55415(612) 664-5600
Fax: (612) 664-5787

MISSISSIPPI—NORTHERN DISTRICT
900 Jefferson Avenue
Oxford, MS 38655
(662) 234-3351
Fax: (662) 234-4818

MISSISSIPPI—SOUTHERN DISTRICT
One Jackson Place
188 East Capitol Street, Suite 500
Jackson, MS 39201
(601) 965-4480
Fax: (601) 965-4409

MISSOURI—EASTERN DISTRICT
U.S. Courthouse
111 South Tenth Street, Room 20.333
St. Louis, MO 63102
(314) 539-2200
Fax: (314) 539-2309

MISSOURI—WESTERN DISTRICT
Charles E. Whitaker Courthouse
400 East Ninth Street, 5th Floor
Kansas City, MO 64106-2149
(816) 426-3122
Fax: (816) 426-4210

MONTANA
P.O. Box 1478
Billings, MT 59103
(406) 657-6101
Fax: (406) 657-6989

NEBRASKA
1620 Dodge Street, Suite 1400
Omaha, NE 68102
(402) 661-3700
Fax: (402) 661-3080

NEVADA
333 Las Vegas Boulevard, Suite 5000
Las Vegas, Nevada 89101
 (702) 388-6336
Fax: (702) 388-6296

NEW HAMPSHIRE
55 Pleasant Street, Room 352
Concord, NH 03301-3904
(603) 225-1552
Fax: (603) 225-1470

NEW JERSEY
Peter Rodino Federal Building
970 Broad Street, Room 700
Newark, NJ 07102
(973) 645-2700
Fax: (973) 645-2702

NEW MEXICO
P.O. Box 607
Albuquerque, NM 87103
(505) 346-7274
Fax: (505) 346-7296

NEW YORK—EASTERN DISTRICT
U.S. Courthouse
147 Pierrepont Street
Brooklyn, NY 11201
(718) 254-7000
Fax: (718) 254-6479

NEW YORK—NORTHERN DISTRICT
James M. Hanley Federal Building
100 South Clinton Street, Room 900
Syracuse, NY 13261
 (315) 448-0672
Fax: (315) 448-0689

NEW YORK—SOUTHERN DISTRICT
One St. Andrews Plaza
New York, NY 10007
(212) 637-2200
Fax: (212) 637-2611

NEW YORK—WESTERN DISTRICT
138 Delaware Avenue
Buffalo, NY 14202
(716) 843-5700
Fax: (716) 551-3052

NORTH CAROLINA—EASTERN DISTRICT
Federal Building
310 New Bern Avenue, Suite 800
Raleigh, NC 27601-1461
(919) 856-4530
Fax: (919) 856-4487

NORTH CAROLINA—MIDDLE DISTRICT
P.O. Box 1858
Greensboro, NC 27402
(336) 333-5351
Fax: (336) 333-5438

NORTH CAROLINA—WESTERN DISTRICT
Carillon Building
227 West Trade Street, Suite 1650
Charlotte, NC 28202
(704) 344-6222
Fax: (704) 344-6629

NORTH DAKOTA
Quentin N. Burdick U.S. Courthouse
655 First Avenue North, Suite 250
Fargo, ND 58102
(701) 297-7400
Fax: (701) 297-7405

OHIO—NORTHERN DISTRICT
801 West Superior Avenue, Suite 400
Cleveland, OH 44113
(216) 622-3600
Fax: (216) 522-3370

OHIO—SOUTHERN DISTRICT
Federal Building
200 West Second Street, Suite 400
Dayton, OH 45402
(937) 225-2910
Fax: (937) 225-2564

OKLAHOMA—EASTERN DISTRICT
1200 West Okmulgee Street
Muskogee, OK 74401
(918) 684-5100
Fax: (918) 684-5130

OKLAHOMA—NORTHERN DISTRICT
110 West Seventh Street, Suite 300
Tulsa, OK 74119(918) 382-2700
Fax: (918) 560-7938

OKLAHOMA—WESTERN DISTRICT
First Oklahoma Tower
210 Park Avenue, Suite 400
Oklahoma City, OK 73102
(405) 553-8700
Fax: (405) 553-8888

OREGON
1000 Southwest Third Avenue, Suite 600
Portland, OR 97204
(503) 727-1000
Fax: (503) 727-1117

PENNSYLVANIA—EASTERN DISTRICT
Philadelphia Life Building
615 Chestnut Street, Suite 1250
Philadelphia, PA 19106-4476
(215) 861-8200
Fax: (215) 861-8609

PENNSYLVANIA—MIDDLE DISTRICT
PO Box 309Scranton, PA 18501
(570) 348-2800
Fax: (570) 348-2816

PENNSYLVANIA—WESTERN DISTRICT
U.S. Post Office and Courthouse Building
700 Grant Street, Room 633
Pittsburgh, PA 15219
(412) 644-3500
Fax: (412) 644-4549

PUERTO RICO
Torre Chardon, Suite 1201
350 Carlos Chardon Avenue
San Juan, PR 00918
(787) 766-5656
Fax: (787) 766-6219

RHODE ISLAND
Fleet Center
50 Kennedy Plaza, 8th Floor
Providence, RI 02903
(401) 709-5000
Fax: (401) 709-5001

SOUTH CAROLINA
First Union Building
1441 Main Street, Suite 500
Columbia, SC 29201
(803) 929-3000
Fax: (803) 254-2912

SOUTH DAKOTA
P.O. Box 3303
Sioux Falls, SD 57101-3303
(605) 330-4400
Fax: (605) 330-4410

TENNESSEE—EASTERN DISTRICT
800 Market Street, Suite 211
Knoxville, TN 37902
(865) 545-4167
Fax: (865) 545-4176

TENNESSEE—MIDDLE DISTRICT
110 Ninth Avenue South, Suite A-961
Nashville TN 37203
(615) 736-5151
Fax: (615) 736—5323

TENNESSEE—WESTERN DISTRICT
Davis Federal Building
167 North Main Street, Room 820
Memphis, TN 38103
(901) 544-4231
Fax: (901) 544-4230

TEXAS—EASTERN DISTRICT
350 Magnolia Avenue, Suite 150
Beaumont, TX 77701
(409) 839-2538
Fax: (409) 839-2550

TEXAS—NORTHERN DISTRICT
Earl Cabell Federal Building
1100 Commerce Street, 3rd Floor
Dallas, TX 75242
(214) 659-8600
Fax: (214) 767-2898

TEXAS—SOUTHERN DISTRICT
P.O. Box 61129
Houston, TX 77208
(713) 567-9000
Fax: (713) 718-3300

TEXAS—WESTERN DISTRICT
601 Northwest Loop 410, Suite 600
San Antonio, TX 78216
(210) 384-7100
Fax: (210) 384-7105

UTAH
185 South State Street, Suite 300
Salt Lake City, UT 84111
(801) 524-5682
Fax: (801) 524-6924

VERMONT
Federal Building
P.O. Box 570
Burlington, VT 05402
(802) 951-6725
Fax: (802) 951-6540

VIRGIN ISLANDS
Federal Building and U.S. Courthouse
5500 Veterans Drive, Room 260
St. Thomas, VI 00802-6424
(340) 774-5757
Fax: (340) 776-3474

VIRGINIA—EASTERN DISTRICT
2100 Jamieson Avenue
Alexandria, VA 22314
(703) 299-3700
Fax: (703) 299-2584

VIRGINIA—WESTERN DISTRICT
310 First Street, SW, Room 901
Roanoke, VA 24011
 (540) 857-2250
Fax: (540) 857-2614

WASHINGTON—EASTERN DISTRICT
Federal Courthouse
P.O. Box 1494
Spokane, WA 99210-1494
(509) 353-2767
Fax: (509) 353-2766

WASHINGTON—WESTERN DISTRICT
700 Stewart Street, Suite 5220
Seattle, WA 98101
(206) 553-7970
Fax: (206) 553-0882

WEST VIRGINIA—NORTHERN DISTRICT
P.O. Box 591
Wheeling, WV 26003
(304) 234-0100
Fax: (304) 234-0110

WEST VIRGINIA—SOUTHERN DISTRICT
P.O. Box 1713
Charleston, WV 25326
(304) 345-2200
Fax: (304) 347-7074

WISCONSIN—EASTERN DISTRICT
Henry S. Reuss Federal Building
517 East Wisconsin Avenue, Room 530
Milwaukee, WI 53202
(414) 297-1700
Fax: (414) 297-1738

WISCONSIN—WESTERN DISTRICT
P.O. Box 1585
Madison, WI 53701-1585
(608) 264-5158
Fax: (608) 264-5172

WYOMING
P.O. Box 668
Cheyenne, WY 82003-0668
(307) 772-2124
Fax: (307) 772-2123

U.S. COMMISSION ON CIVIL RIGHTS REGIONAL OFFICES
Address Complaints to: Regional Director

EASTERN REGIONAL OFFICE
Area Covered: Connecticut, Delaware, District of Columbia, Maine, Maryland, Massachusetts, New Hampshire, New Jersey, New York, Pennsylvania, Rhode Island, Vermont, Virginia, and West Virginia
624 Ninth Street, NW, Suite 740
Washington, DC 20425
(202) 376-7533
TTY: (202) 376-8116
Fax: (202) 376-7548

SOUTHERN REGIONAL OFFICE
Area Covered: Florida, Georgia, Kentucky, North Carolina, South Carolina, and Tennessee
61 Forsyth Street, SW, Suite 1840T
Atlanta, GA 30303
(404) 562-7000
TTY: (404) 562-7004
Fax: (404) 562-7005

MIDWESTERN REGIONAL OFFICE
Area Covered: Illinois, Indiana, Michigan, Minnesota, Ohio, and Wisconsin
55 West Monroe Street, Suite 410
Chicago, IL 60603
(312) 353-8311
TTY: (312) 353-8362
Fax: (312) 353-8324

CENTRAL REGIONAL OFFICE
Area Covered: Alabama, Arkansas, Iowa, Kansas, Louisiana, Mississippi, Missouri, Nebraska, and Oklahoma
400 State Avenue, Suite 908
Kansas City, KS 66101
(913) 551-1400
TTY: (913) 551-1414
Fax: (913) 551-1413

ROCKY MOUNTAIN REGIONAL OFFICE
Area Covered: Colorado, Montana, New Mexico, North Dakota, South Dakota, Utah, and Wyoming
1961 Stout Street, Suite 240
Denver, CO 80294
(303) 866-1040
TTY: (303) 866-1049
Fax: (303) 866-1050

WESTERN REGIONAL OFFICE
Area Covered: Alaska, Arizona, California, Hawaii, Idaho, Nevada, Oregon, Texas, and Washington
300 North Los Angeles Street, Suite 2010
Los Angeles, CA 90012
(213) 894-3437
TTY: (213) 894-3435
Fax: (213) 894-0508

U.S. COMMISSION ON CIVIL RIGHTS
Washington, DC 20425

Visit us on the Web:
www.usccr.gov